CHRIST-CENTERED PARENTING

GOSPEL CONVERSATIONS ON COMPLEX CULTURAL ISSUES

**RUSSELL MOORE &
PHILLIP BETHANCOURT**

LifeWay Press® Nashville, Tennessee

Published by LifeWay Press® • ©2017 Ethics and Religious Liberty Commission

No part of this book may be reproduced or transmitted in any form or by any means, electronic or mechanical, including photocopying and recording, or by any information storage or retrieval system, except as may be expressly permitted in writing by the publisher. Requests for permission should be addressed in writing to LifeWay Press®; One LifeWay Plaza; Nashville, TN 37234-0152.

ISBN 978-1-4300-6335-3
Item 005790851
Dewey decimal classification: 649
Subject heading: PARENTING \ POPULAR CULTURE \ CHRISTIAN ETHICS

Unless otherwise noted, Scripture quotations are from the Christian Standard Bible®, copyright ©2017 by Holman Bible Publishers. Used by permission. Christian Standard Bible® and CSB® are federally registered trademarks of Holman Bible Publishers. Scripture quotations marked ESV have been taken from the ESV® Bible (The Holy Bible, English Standard Version®), copyright ©2001 by Crossway, a publishing ministry of Good News Publishers. Used by permission. All rights reserved.

To order additional copies of this resource, write LifeWay Church Resources Customer Service; One LifeWay Plaza; Nashville, TN 37234-0113; FAX order to 615.251.5933; call toll-free 800.458.2772; email orderentry@lifeway.com; order online at LifeWay.com; or visit the LifeWay Christian Store serving you.

Printed in the United States of America.

Adult Ministry Publishing, LifeWay Church Resources, One LifeWay Plaza, Nashville, TN 37234-0152

CONTENTS

ABOUT THE AUTHORS

RUSSELL MOORE

Russell Moore is president of the Ethics & Religious Liberty Commission of the Southern Baptist Convention, the moral and public policy agency of the nation's largest Protestant denomination. He is a frequent cultural commentator, an ethicist, and theologian. The Wall Street Journal has called him "vigorous, cheerful, and fiercely articulate." Moore is the author of several books, including *Onward: Engaging the Culture without Losing the Gospel*. A native Mississippian, he and his wife Maria are the parents of five boys.

PHILLIP BETHANCOURT

Phillip Bethancourt is the Executive Vice President of the ERLC. He is also Assistant Professor of Christian Theology at The Southern Baptist Theological Seminary and on the Pastoral Leadership Team at Redemption City Church in Franklin, Tennessee. He and his wife, Cami, have four boys: Nathan, Lawson, Weston, and Hudson.

ERLC STAFF & VIDEO PANEL HOSTS

DANIEL DARLING

Daniel Darling is Vice President of Communications for the ERLC. He and his wife, Angela, have four children and live in the Nashville, Tennessee, area. He is the author of several books and is a contributing editor to Christianity Today's *CT Pastors*.

DANIEL PATTERSON

Daniel Patterson serves as Vice President of Operations and Chief of Staff at the ERLC. He and his wife, Molly, have been married since 2010, and together they have two daughters, Emma and Claire.

ANDREW T. WALKER

Andrew T. Walker serves as Director of Policy Studies with the ERLC. He is married to Christian, and they have two daughters, Caroline and Catherine.

VIDEO PANELISTS

TRILLIA NEWBELL

Trillia Newbell is the Director of Community Outreach for the ERLC. She is the author of four books, including the children's book, *God's Very Good Idea*. Trillia is married to her best friend, Thern, and they reside with their two children near Nashville, Tennessee.

RAY ORTLUND

Ray Ortlund is pastor of Immanuel Church, Nashville, Tennessee, an Acts 29 church. Ray has been married to Jani for forty-five years. They have four grown children and thirteen grandchildren—so far!

JACKIE HILL PERRY

Jackie Hill Perry is a writer and artist. She is married to Preston Perry, and they have a daughter named Eden.

DAVID E. PRINCE

David E. Prince is pastor of preaching and vision at Ashland Avenue Baptist Church in Lexington, Kentucky, and assistant professor of Christian preaching at The Southern Baptist Theological Seminary. He is married to Judi and they have eight children (three boys and five girls).

BEN STUART

Ben Stuart serves on the team at Passion City Church in Atlanta, Georgia, and is preparing to launch and pastor a Passion City Church location in Washington, D.C. Ben is the author of *Single, Dating, Engaged, Married* and lives in Atlanta with his wife, Donna, and their three children.

JEN WILKIN

Jen Wilkin is a wife, mom to four, and an advocate for Christians to love God with their minds through the faithful study of His Word. She is an author and Bible teacher, and currently serves on staff with The Village Church Institute.

INTRODUCTION

Each day, as you do the very ordinary work of being moms and dads, you are teaching your kids how to live. The work of parenting has always been challenging, but today we face the added pressure of raising our children in a world that barely resembles the one we grew up in. If you are like us, you are well aware of just how ill-equipped you are for the task.

There is some good news. Our most basic problems are the same ones we have always faced. We are sinful beings in a fallen world. The good news is that through the gospel, Jesus has redeemed us from sin and is making all things new.

Christ redeemed us from the curse of the law by becoming a curse for us, because it is written, Cursed is everyone who is hung on a tree.
GALATIANS 3:13

Then the one seated on the throne said, "Look, I am making everything new." He also said, "Write, because these words are faithful and true."
REVELATION 21:5

You will find that this entire study is based on a simple idea. When Christ is the foundation for your parenting, it enables you to equip your children to navigate even the most complex issues in the culture today.

We know the world is changing at breakneck speed. We know you cannot possibly keep up with it. But what you can do is be there for your kids. You can follow the Bible's admonition to instruct them in the fear and knowledge of the Lord as you walk alongside them each day.

Listen, Israel: The LORD our God, the LORD is one. LORD the LORD your God with all your heart, with all your soul, and with all your strength. These words that I am giving you today are to be in your heart. Repeat them to your children. Talk about them when you sit in your house and when you walk along the road, when you lie down and when you get up. Bind them as a sign on your hand and let them be a symbol on your forehead. Write them on the doorposts of your house and on your city gates.
DEUTERONOMY 6:4-9

This study is intended to equip you to face the challenges presented by the culture. As the world around us continues to shift and become more secular, this curriculum will help prepare you and your children to meet these moral and ethical challenges. At times, we will encourage you to talk together about difficult and sensitive issues. Don't be afraid. Your child will be better equipped to face these things if you are there to shape and guide their thinking.

Picking up this study is a step in that direction. It is our prayer that God will use it to assist you as you continue doing one of the most important tasks of your entire life. Children are a stewardship and a precious heritage from the Lord.

Sons are indeed a heritage from the LORD,
offspring, a reward.
PSALM 127:3

They need you more than you know. May God bless you as you seek to honor Him in your parenting.

FOR THE KINGDOM,

Russell Moore and Phillip Bethancourt

HOW TO USE THIS STUDY

Welcome to *Christ-Centered Parenting*. This six-session study will help equip parents of children, youth, and young adults to navigate difficult and complex cultural issues that face our families today.

This study is designed to be used in a weekly small-group setting of parents. However, it can also be used with larger groups, as an individual study, as well as a resource for those who work with children, youth, young adults, and their parents.

The study consists of the following components:

1. VIDEO

Each video session is approximately 30 minutes and features a panel discussion on how to parent in the midst of a specific complex cultural issue. Each panel is hosted by a member of the ERLC staff and includes Russell Moore with other knowledgeable guests. The panelists come from different walks of life and ministry, but have this in common— they are all parents.

There is a Viewer Guide page provided for you to take notes on the video content.

2. GROUP DISCUSSION

Following the video, several questions are provided on the Group Guide pages to help your group discuss the session issue. Also, there is a Takeaways section at the end of the Group Guide for you to jot down notes to remember or list what you've learned from the video and group discussion.

3. ARTICLES

Each session contains three articles that deal with one facet of the larger issue discussed on the video and in your small group. These articles are to be read between sessions. There are reflection questions at the end of each article to help you process and apply the information. Also, you can use these questions to discuss the article with your spouse or other parents.

4. AGE-GRADED INFORMATION SHEETS

Following the articles are information sheets for six age-graded categories: preschoolers, younger elementary kids, pre-teens, middle schoolers, high schoolers, and young adults. The sheets will give you a brief overview of where most children are concerning that session's specific issue. Understand that this is general information and will not apply to every specific situation you face with your child. We encourage you to go to the age range your child or student is in to see what is generally recommended for most kids his or her age. Check the age group before and after to see what is most suitable for your child according to his or her level of growth, development, and Bible knowledge. Learning style and pace will differ from child to child. Precise ages are not given because God designed each child to develop differently. Your child will progress through Bible concepts and life application unique to how God created your child and his or her knowledge of and interaction with the Bible.

Here are the elements found on each age-graded page:

KEY SCRIPTURES

This is not an exhaustive list of Scripture that applies to each issue, but a starting point for you to reference. You can use these Scripture passages in your personal study or family devotions as you talk about these issues.

KEY QUESTIONS

We have provided a short list of questions your child might ask concerning the issues at hand.

AT THIS AGE ...

These are some things most children are dealing with, thinking about, or experiencing at each specific age.

DEVELOPMENTAL MILESTONES

This list could include emotional, social, physical, or spiritual milestones they will have attained by or will attain during this age.

COACHING TIPS

These are brief parenting tips to encourage, challenge, and equip you to be a better parent during this age.

CONVERSATION STARTERS

We have provided a list of simple questions to help prompt conversations between you and your child.

SAY OR PRAY

This is a list of encouraging words or prayer prompts specific to the session issue.

SESSION 1
GOSPEL FRAMEWORK

ALLOWING THE GOSPEL TO
SHAPE YOUR PARENTING

Use the space below to record notes, quotes, thoughts, and questions from the video panel discussion.

_____
_____
_____
_____
_____
_____
_____
_____
_____
_____
_____
_____
_____
_____
_____
_____
_____
_____
_____
_____
_____
_____
_____
_____
_____
_____
_____
_____
_____

Use the following questions and prompts to continue the conversation about the issues discussed by the video panel.

How do you define "gospel"?

How does the gospel influence the decision making in your home?

What are the effects of performance-based love on our children? How can we stop this and move toward unconditional love?

What can we learn from the parable of the prodigal son (Luke 15:11-32) about gospel-based parenting?

How do you incorporate law and grace in your home?

Why does your home need to be a safe place to fail? Is that how you would describe your home currently? Explain.

Are you vulnerable with your children? Are you honest about your failures? Do they see repentance in you? Why is this so important?

Would you say the boundaries for your children are too stiff? Too lax? Just right? Explain.

Would you call yourself a distracted parent? Why or why not? What's the worst distraction for you?

Name some of the broken families in the Bible. What issues did they deal with? Why is it important to remember that we are all broken?

What are the repercussions of continually comparing your family to the ideal?

How are you maintaining a culture of communication and conversation in your home?

TAKEAWAYS:

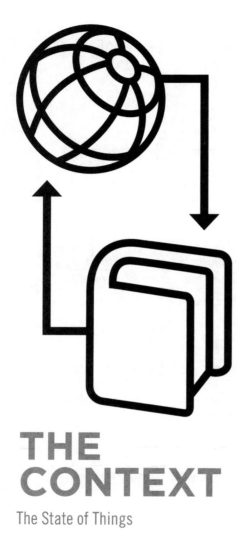

THE CONTEXT

The State of Things

> The Christian church in the West now faces a set of challenges that exceeds anything it has experienced in the past. [This] is a revolution more subtle and more dangerous than revolutions faced in previous generations. This is a revolution of ideas—one that is transforming the entire moral structure of meaning and life that human beings have recognized for millennia.[1]
> **DR. ALBERT MOHLER**

Consider the issue of human sexuality. Americans' beliefs about same-sex marriage have undergone seismic shifts in a matter of decades. What was almost completely taboo thirty years ago is now not only culturally acceptable but legally protected and celebrated. The Internet makes pornography easily accessible for even the youngest of children. Some public schools have become ground zero for introducing progressive sexual ethics. And the list goes on. How can Christian parents meet the challenges of this cultural moment? Perhaps your kids have already decided where they stand on the big issues. Or perhaps there is a war raging in their heads as they listen to all the different voices telling them what to believe. Either way, parents cannot afford to be silent.

TWO SIDES OF THE ROAD

As we navigate this narrow road of Christ-centered parenting, we are in danger of falling to extremes. On one side is the temptation to bow to the culture and conform. Unfortunately, far too many well-intentioned Christian parents have unwittingly found themselves in this very ditch (or at least they would, if they took the time to notice),

Every generation has faced challenges in parenting. As the culture shifts, long-standing beliefs are put to the test, and Christians are often left wondering how they are to remain faithful in the new normal.

At the same time, there is no denying that Christian parents today face unique challenges in the midst of a culture that continues to put a wedge between itself and the teachings of the Bible.

Conformity
Legalism

and this is easy to understand. Parents face near-constant pressure to adopt the habits and beliefs of the prevailing culture when it comes to raising children. While this pressure is often subtle—it just seems easier not to go against the grain—it is always insidious. We must not be fooled. The truth of Scripture does not change. As Paul urged in Romans 12,

Do not be conformed to this age, but be transformed by the renewing of your mind, so that you may discern what is the good, pleasing, and perfect will of God.
ROMANS 12:2

The only conforming we are to do as Christ-followers is that of our minds to His perfect will.

On the other side of the road is legalism. This is nothing new. Even some who saw Jesus in the flesh were guilty of falling into this ditch. The Pharisees, in their relentless effort to keep every part of God's law down to the letter, added additional expectations to every God-given rule. If the law commanded to do no work on the Sabbath, they extended this to mean you could not lift a finger to help a friend in need. Jesus rebuked the Pharisees in Matthew 23 saying that while they kept the law externally, their hearts were far from God.

A Pharisaical approach to parenting means we build up walls of protection around our kids. It is a system built on rules rather than relationship and on fear rather than faith. While that may keep our children safe in the short-term, it does not equip them with a long-term battle plan on how to engage a culture that will continue to change throughout their lifetime.

The struggle to navigate the road between these two ditches is one of the true challenges of Christ-centered parenting. On the one hand, we always want to raise our children with the right values and to be the right kind of people. While on the other hand, we desperately want to teach our children to love people and make a difference in the world. Because of our humanness and limitations, we are regularly tempted to steer too strongly in one direction or the other. Most conservative evangelicals are readily aware of the danger of too much immersion in the culture. It can easily influence our kids away from God. So we go to great lengths to avoid this danger in our homes and in our churches. Surely it is good to recognize that parents function as the curators of what influences the young minds God has entrusted to us. But even so, it is the other, more subtle danger that should cause us the greatest concern. If we aren't careful and vigilant, we may be guilty of raising up little Pharisees who so imbibe the values we teach that they begin to use them as a weapon with which to judge others.

THE FAMILY DISCIPLESHIP UNIT

As we confront the complexities of our culture in the midst of raising our children, we can't fall to one side or the other, and we can't shut down. Shutting down says to our kids that we are afraid of these issues. It says these are the things we don't want to talk about. If we as Christian parents think we will be able to escape or wait out these drastic culture changes, hoping the pendulum will eventually swing back, we are mistaken. Cultural progressivism does not have a fixed destination.[2] This trajectory will continue, and silence is not an option—we must engage.

Unless we are actively discipling our kids, the world will disciple them for us. We cannot let the responsibility of parenting fall to the culture or to the schools. We cannot even let it fall primarily to the church, although the church should be our closest partner. If we are merely sending our kids down the church hall twice a week for Sunday School and youth group meetings, while failing to teach them the truths of Scripture in our own home, then we are guilty of forsaking our God-given role as parents. Hoping they hear it from someone else isn't good enough. God's design has always been for faith instruction to take place primarily within the family. See Moses' instruction to the Israelites in Deuteronomy 6:

Listen, Israel: The LORD our God, the LORD is one. Love the LORD your God with all your heart, with all your soul, and with all your strength. These words that I am giving you today are to be in your heart. Repeat them to your children. Talk about them when you sit in your house and when you walk along the road, when you lie down and when you get up. Bind them as a sign on your hand and let them be a symbol on your forehead.

God's Word is our best weapon in this battle. His Word is our anchor in the confusing culture of tolerance and relativism. But we can't teach to our children what we don't live and know. We must spend time in God's Word. The Scriptures instruct us to pass the faith along to our kids by intentionally and regularly repeating God's words to them. We must look for ways in the everyday moments of life to speak of the gospel and point our kids to Jesus. We must seek out opportunities to speak God's Word to them.

What better discipleship unit than the family? What better model, teacher, and shepherd over a little one than a parent? God's desire for your family is to be a Trinity-displaying, God-glorifying, disciple-making unit. God gives us little children so that we can influence them to become fully devoted followers of Jesus Christ who love Him and love others. It is messy and inefficient, rewarding and frustrating, and ultimately, profoundly glorious work.[3]
CHAP BETTIS

The good news is we're not alone in these muddy waters. The responsibility of Christ-centered parenting falls on each of us, but thankfully it doesn't depend solely on us. We have a heavenly Father who gave the gift of the Holy Spirit who is with us forever and will teach us all things (John 14:16,26). We have the truth of Scripture to guide and sharpen us (2 Tim. 3:16-17). We have each other, the church of Jesus Christ.

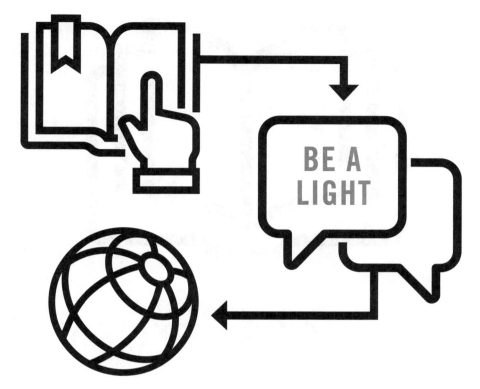

The worst thing we could do is follow that familiar advice to "pray as if it all depended on God, and work as if it all depended on you." Rather, we need to become people who work as if it all depends on God—because it does, and because that is the best possible news. We work for, indeed work in the life and power of, a gracious and infinitely resourceful Creator, Redeemer, and Sustainer. And we need to know ourselves well enough that the thought that it might in fact all depend on us would drive us straight to fasting and trembling prayer.[4]
ANDY CROUCH

On your knees is not a bad place to begin this journey. Pray for our fallen world that those who are far from Christ would be reconciled to Him. Pray for your kids as they venture every day into a culture that opposes the message of the cross. Pray for strength from the Lord to fulfill your role in training your children in the way of truth.

QUESTIONS FOR REFLECTION

1. How does our changing culture most challenge you as a parent?
   resisting conforming

2. Would you say you lean more toward conforming or legalism?

3. In what ways are you actively discipling your child?
   example + scripture

4. What one thing stood out to you from this article?
   Two sides of the road conformity + legalism

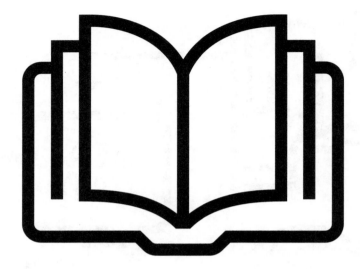

THE GOSPEL STORY

The gospel is not only a message of salvation for those apart from Christ. It is the foundation and hope of our parenting. And we know this is true because the gospel itself is the story of our heavenly Father reconciling His children to Himself through the work of His Son.

Allowing the gospel to shape and inform our approach to parenting will cause us to think differently. Consider this example: In our practice of parenting, we often act as though our child's relationship with God is completely up to us. This can result in our sincere attempts to lead our children to faith to become awkward or overbearing.

So why do Christian parents feel so much pressure to produce Christian offspring?

Train up a child in the way he should go; even when he is old he will not depart from it.
PROVERBS 22:6, ESV

At first glance, Proverbs seems to offer us an ironclad promise: Raise your children "the right way," and they will automatically "turn out right." Perhaps you've heard sermons or Bible study lessons insist that this is the message of Proverbs 22:6. But telling parents that the solution to having Christian kids solely depends on their ability to train them up is not only unfair to parents, it is unfair to the Scriptures.

Proverbs 22:6 was never written to serve as a stand-alone foundation for the biblical model of parenting. Yes, parents have a God-ordained responsibility to raise their children in the fear and admonition of the Lord. But this verse from Proverbs (as well as the entire book) presents us with wisdom, not a formula.

Sadly, misreading and misapplying this verse has led many Christian mothers and fathers to embrace a humanistic, results-oriented approach to parenting. Instead, when we see Proverbs 22:6 embedded within the gospel story, it enables us to depend on Jesus rather than ourselves in our parenting.

Putting all the pressure on parents to execute and then blaming only them for failure is both unbiblical and impossible—unbiblical because it removes the work of God and brings glory to man; impossible because human parents cannot manufacture what only the Holy Spirit can produce.

We also forget that every child is an individual human soul, created with their own accountability before God. Worse, we ignore the work of the Holy Spirit in the shaping of a child's soul.

So what is the job of a Christian parent? Faithfulness. Parents are given the task of creating a culture of faith that intentionally uses all of life to point their children toward a lifelong relationship with God. We're to equip them for life.

Yet the job of salvation and spiritual growth can only be done by God through the work of the Holy Spirit. Only God can shape the human heart. Only God can call us out of sin and give us life. Too many Christian parenting models operate under the subtle assumption that the life, death, and resurrection of Jesus Christ is incidental to parenting. But gospel parenting is about much more than raising moral children. It is about constantly pointing our children to Jesus with our words and with our lives. Even so, the

Parents are given the task of creating a culture of faith that intentionally uses all of life to point their children toward a lifelong relationship with God.

beauty of gospel parenting is that it frees us from taking the place of God.

In a gospel paradigm, parents are both evangelists and disciple-makers, continually retelling the story of creation, man's sin, Jesus' offer of redemption, and the promise of the Holy Spirit in guiding their children toward their God-given purpose. We earnestly pray with fervent trust, knowing that it is the Father, Son, and Holy Spirit who will do the work of creating faith in our children and making them more like Jesus.

Children are a divine stewardship. They are not for us to own but for us to love, carefully guide, and then release to God's providential care. We cannot pressure, bully, or force them into faith. We parent, not with anticipation of some promised outcome, but out of faithfulness to Jesus, leaving the outcome to Him.

THE CULTURE

Gospel parenting puts God at the center of our parenting—not our own efforts and not our children. This approach reframes the predominant message of the culture that elevates the experience of the individual, turning our energy and attention inward—on self. The prevailing culture presents a paradigm of moral relativism where each person is free, even encouraged to define for themselves what is right and wrong. The world proclaims, "Be true to yourself. Follow your heart and your desires. What's right for you is right for you."

A short walk through Scripture reveals the fallacy in this mind-set.

The heart is deceitful above all things, and desperately sick; who can understand it?
JEREMIAH 17:9, ESV

All a person's ways seem right to him, but the LORD weighs hearts.
PROVERBS 21:2

In those days there was no king in Israel; everyone did whatever seemed right to him.
JUDGES 21:25

This verse in Judges follows a lengthy description of the tribe of Benjamin's departure from following the law and their refusal to recognize the Lord as their King. They traded the one true God, who called them and set them apart, for fleeting earthly desires and self-reliance. Just as Paul says of the ungodly, the cultural paradigm of *self first* exchanges "the truth of God for a lie" (Rom. 1:25). It trades the authority of God for sin and perceived autonomy.

This exchange started in the garden when God's first man and woman, created in His image, chose what they felt was best for them over God's plan. But the gospel is a call to repentance, turning from sin and turning to Christ. Our old self is crucified with Him and we are raised up to walk in a new way of life, free from the enslavement of sin (Rom. 6:4-7). Paul says,

I no longer live, but Christ lives in me. The life I now live in the body, I live by faith in the Son of God, who loved me and gave himself for me.
GALATIANS 2:20

WHERE TO BEGIN

So our lives are not our own, just as our children's lives are not their own. We are created in "the image of God" (Gen. 1:27) and now as Christians our lives are "hidden with Christ" (Col. 3:3). So now our ambition is not to elevate our own desires but to follow after the heart of God. As parents, our aim with our kids is not simply to build up their self-esteem but to help them see their utter dependence on God. The biggest challenge every parent faces is not their kids' behavior but their sin. A Christ-centered approach to parenting recognizes we are sinners raising sinners.

Coming to Jesus means we stop using our hearts as the beginning point for determining what is right and wrong, submitting instead to His Word.[5]
J.D. GREEAR

Our starting point for gospel conversations with our kids is the message of the gospel woven through Scripture. We address complex cultural issues with the authority of God's Word, rather than the instability of our own thoughts and feelings. The Bible is our guide for godly living.

Taking the Bible as our starting point is a demonstration of humility. It means we stop relying on our own wisdom and lean fully into the grace and mercy of Jesus. We confess our own dependence upon our heavenly Father, and we cease to parent out of fear or insecurity. In our weak and sinful state, God sent His Son to die for us (Rom. 5:6-8). As parents, we must always be mindful of our weakness and insufficiency. We must rely on God and point our children back to Him.

The story of our sin and the redemption found only in Christ transforms every aspect of our lives. As we parent with the gospel in focus, we will let go of earthly desires, prioritizing instead the things of Christ and His kingdom. We will understand how to love, how to parent, and how to live when we shine the light of the gospel into every corner of our lives. The love of

our heavenly Father gives us a model for loving the children He has entrusted to us. God's Word gives us a standard by which to discern truth versus falsehood.

Being rooted in the gospel equips us to navigate the complex challenges of culture, challenges we are otherwise unprepared to meet. By immersing ourselves in the gospel, we will parent differently.

QUESTIONS FOR REFLECTION

1. Do you ever feel the pressure to produce Christian offspring? Explain.

2. How does knowing that the salvation and spiritual growth of your children are God's work through His Holy Spirit bring a sense of freedom and peace? How do you see God at work in your children to bring this about?

3. What is your responsibility in Christ-centered parenting? How are you fulfilling that responsibility?

4. What one thing stood out to you from this article?

THE MISSION

INTO THE WORLD

As Christianity grows more estranged from the mainstream of American culture, we will be forced to relearn the distinction between the church and the world. We are "strangers and exiles" in this world, urged "to abstain from sinful desires that wage war against the soul" (1 Pet. 2:11), but we should not assume that means isolation or disengagement from the culture. Jesus made this clear to His disciples in John 17. He prayed for them, acknowledging that the world would hate them because they were not "of the world" (v. 14). But Jesus did not want them to be taken out of the world. Instead, He prayed for them to be sent into the world, just as He was sent (v. 18). Rather than disassociating themselves from the world, the disciples were sent into the world with a mission. This distinction

is crucial for parents. We can neither embrace a culture that is in opposition to the teachings of Jesus, nor hide away from a world that Christ came to redeem.

This can present a real challenge for parents as we teach our kids about culture. Here are two common mistakes we should avoid:

1) WE OVEREXPOSE OUR KIDS TO THE CULTURE. The Bible doesn't use the term, "culture," but it does use a very similar word, "world." This is a loose definition of the prevailing thinking in a given society. Typically the values of the culture run counter to the way of Christ, but not always. Sometimes a culture is shaped by Christian influence. Parents should be cautious in what we allow our kids to embrace. We cannot afford to be passive, allowing them to form ungodly convictions based on what everyone else is thinking and saying. Media and relationships are forms of culture that pose particular challenges for parents. We must be wise in monitoring the media our children consume, how much time they spend online, and the amount of time they spend with friends (not to mention who their friends are).

2) WE UNDEREXPOSE OUR KIDS TO THE CULTURE. This is the opposite danger to overexposure. It is easy to adopt a fortress mentality as parents, sheltering our kids so much from the world that they have no ability to discern truth from error or ugliness from beauty. There is a tendency to overprotect our kids so much that we fail to prepare them for their mission in this world. Our kids will one day live as adults and will require the necessary skills, both spiritual and social, to make wise choices. If our only parenting mode is protection, we fail to teach them how to apply the Scriptures to the reality of life in a sinful world. We cannot do all of their thinking for them. We must give them space to fail and learn and figure out what they did wrong. In the back of our minds we have to remember that we're not simply training our children to be good or protecting them from evil; we're equipping them for God's unique mission in their generation.[6]

These two ideas—protecting and equipping—always exist in tension with each other. As those who are in the world but not of the world, we are right to protect and set proper boundaries. God's Word instructs us:

Renounce ungodliness and worldly passions, and ... live self-controlled, upright, and godly lives in the present age.
TITUS 2:12, ESV

But because we are also sent into the world, we must equip our kids to be on mission for the gospel.

SAFETY IS A MYTH

We live in a world of immense human conflict—war, terrorism, school shootings. The world is unpredictable, and the idea that we could protect our kids from every evil thing is a placid myth at best and a destructive lie at worst. If we are truly basing our approach to parenting on the gospel, then we should raise the banner of the Great Commission as our parenting mantra. Think about this for a moment. What if in a world of warring nations, economic challenges, and many faiths, we equipped our kids to follow the Great Commission:

Make disciples of all nations, baptizing them in the name of the Father and of the Son and of the Holy Spirit, teaching them to observe everything I have commanded you.
MATTHEW 28:19-20

What if we did this, knowing they won't always be safe, but trusting that Jesus is always with them just as He promised?

David Prince, a professor and pastor, writes,

If the gospel is true, a safety-first, safety-centric worldview is a lie. A world where nothing is worth suffering and dying for is a world in which it is difficult to discern what is worth living for. Teach your children that love itself is an aggressive act that is often costly and demands courage. Defending the defenseless, speaking truth in love, and helping those in need, will often put them in harm's way.[7]

Living faithfully in a diverse society means holding fast to the truth of Scripture that Jesus Christ is the only hope for this world, while at the same time loving your neighbor as yourself.

Paul assured his spiritual son Timothy,

All who desire to live a godly life in Christ Jesus will be persecuted.
2 TIMOTHY 3:12, ESV

If we are truly gospel people, we will be motivated to move beyond our safety and comfort to address the issues of our day. Of course we will teach our children about culture from the safety of our homes and churches, but it doesn't stop there. When we shift our efforts from protecting to equipping, our kids will begin to see the world they are called to love through the lens of the gospel. They will see those who are different as neighbors rather than enemies. And they will no longer view the culture as entirely evil, but as a medium through which God's kingdom can advance.

LOVING OUR NEIGHBORS

Living faithfully in a diverse society means holding fast to the truth of Scripture that Jesus Christ is the only hope for this world, while at the same time loving your neighbor as yourself. If we truly live with the gospel as our lens, we will not view the culture as something to be tolerated or despised. We will see a world of people in need of redemption. We will not shy away from difficult conversations, because we will see people at the heart of these conversations, people made in the image of God who are in need of a Savior. Imagine our children caring for victims of human trafficking, speaking up for the unborn, and defending biblical marriage. Imagine them loving "the least of these" (Matt. 25:40)—those in prison, those displaced by the injustices of war, and those friends who are ready to give up on life because they have no hope.

One of the most difficult tensions is raising our children to love sinners on the one hand and yet live their lives in Spirit-directed holiness on the other hand. This is a delicate balance. The best way forward is for us as parents to think about the culture we create in our homes and churches. If your child is trying to determine how to truly love sinners and walk in holiness, he or she will likely begin by looking at you. Our lives should always point our children toward Jesus, His kingdom, and the mission He has given us.

How do we do this? One answer is to constantly have these conversations in our homes. Ask your kids, *What is our mission on this earth? Why are we here? Is our goal to look good or to love others into the kingdom?* Our children are just like us. They need to be reminded of their own desperate need for the gospel all the time; they need to be reminded that the world needs the gospel too, all the time.

Jesus loved sinners. He ate with them, spent time with them, and engaged in long conversations with them. Jesus courageously opposed sin, but His heart was always brimming with love for the world. If we want our children to love like Jesus, we have to love like this too.

We can learn to love others in this way because at the root of our differences, we all have something in common.

For all have sinned and fall short of the glory of God.
ROMANS 3:23

The root of conflict in our world is not our ethnic differences, religious differences, or even our cultural differences. The root of the problem of human conflict is sin. The gospel is an invitation to be reconciled. As those who have been reconciled to Christ and have peace with God, we now are tasked with "the ministry of reconciliation" (2 Cor. 5:18). Mission is a matter of reconciliation, the reconciliation of humanity to God and of humanity with one another.

We are talking about the kingdom of God. We teach our children to participate in the mission of reconciliation because there are millions who do not yet know Jesus as Lord. There will come a day when "every knee will bow … and every tongue will confess that Jesus Christ is Lord" (Phil. 2:10-11) whether they made that confession in this life or not. All will stand before the judgment seat of God to "give an account" (Rom. 14:10-12) and will either spend eternity in communion with Christ or eternity apart from Him. All things will be made known. All differences will be set aside. All wrongs will be made right. May God help us.

QUESTIONS FOR REFLECTION

1. When it comes to exposing your kids to culture, have you tended to overexpose or underexpose? Why?

2. Why is it so important for you to embrace the task of equipping your kids for God's mission? How are you currently doing that?

3. What are the consequences of a "safety-first, safety-centric" worldview when it comes to raising your kids? How can you break out of that view?

4. Is your heart broken for those who don't know Christ? How can you cultivate a love for the lost in your own heart and in the heart of your children?

5. What one thing stood out to you from this article?

BIG IDEA

Raise your child with a biblical framework in a confusing culture that attempts to undermine the gospel.

KEY SCRIPTURES

- *We should obey God because we love Him* (John 14:15).
- *We should train children in the right way* (Prov. 22:6).
- *We should study the Bible* (2 Tim. 2:15).
- *We should tell the world why we love God* (1 Pet. 3:15).
- *We should set an example for the world* (Titus 2:7-8).

KEY QUESTIONS YOUR PRESCHOOLER IS ASKING

- Are Bible stories real or pretend?
- Why can't I see God?
- What does God want me to learn?

AT THIS AGE MOST PRESCHOOLERS WILL …

- Ask countless questions about the world around them.
- Have a limited attention span.
- Think in only literal terms and ideas.

DEVELOPMENTAL MILESTONES

- Preschoolers are ready to learn when their basic physical and emotional needs are met. Some of these needs include love, trust, acceptance, and security. Providing for these essential needs will make children more receptive to the lessons and truths you teach them.
- Because children are literal thinkers and learn through their senses, involving them in hands-on activities can help children remember what they learn, as well as learn how to apply these truths in their lives (with coaching, of course).
- Preschoolers learn largely through relationships and imitation. Their principal source of biblical understanding comes from their parents or teachers. Through your teaching and behavior, you essentially represent God and His Word to your preschooler.

COACHING TIPS

- Repetition is key in shaping a child's mind and teaching him important concepts. He will be a better learner and become more confident about the Bible and its foundational truths. Different approaches to teaching the same concept will also help etch the truth in his heart.
- Building a firm foundation of acceptance and trust will make your preschooler more receptive and keep an open channel of communication between you and your child as she grows. If she trusts you, then she will accept what you teach her as truth despite what she may learn from culture, friends, or media.
- Remember to root every important truth and concept in Scripture. Explain often that God's truth is the only truth, and that it never changes. Talking about these truths often will help kids shape a gospel-centric worldview.

CONVERSATION STARTERS

- **DO YOU REMEMBER WHEN … ?** During casual conversations, reference foundational Bible stories he knows and create a connection between real life and Bible application. For example, if your child mentions that a classmate fell on the playground, discuss the story of the good Samaritan. Ask him how he could act like the good Samaritan at school. Emphasize that we should always show God's love to others.
- **WHO DO YOU KNOW?** When the name of someone you know comes up in conversation, use this as an opportunity to illustrate God's love for people. You can discuss why God loves this person, and bring up ways you can show love to her. Teach your child to see everyone as God sees them.
- **WHY DID I DO THAT?** When you ask your child to do something, such as a chore, ask her why she thinks you wanted her to do it. Discuss why it was important for her to obey, and emphasize the connection between love and obedience. Mention that, in the same way, we obey God's Word because we love Him.

SAY OR PRAY

- God loves us.
- God wants us to obey Him.
- The Bible is true.

BIG IDEA

Raise your child with a biblical framework in a confusing culture that attempts to undermine the gospel.

KEY SCRIPTURES
- *We should obey God because we love Him* (John 14:15).
- *We should train children in the right way* (Prov. 22:6).
- *We should do our best for God* (1 Cor. 10:31).
- *We should tell the world why we love God* (1 Pet. 3:15).
- *We should set an example for the world* (Titus 2:7-8).

KEY QUESTIONS YOUR ELEMENTARY-AGED CHILD IS ASKING
- How can learning what the Bible says help me live?
- Why should I choose to obey God?
- How can I tell other people about God?

AT THIS AGE MOST ELEMENTARY CHILDREN WILL ...
- Be eager to learn how they fit into the world.
- Start taking on responsibilities and facing challenges.
- Begin to think abstractly.

DEVELOPMENTAL MILESTONES
- Children at this age learn best through discovery. Activities involving such things as solving puzzles, taking things apart, and discovering how things are made will help your child engage in and understand the concepts you teach.
- Younger elementary age kids are learning to distinguish between fantasy and reality. Leading your child to understand that God's Word is true and that it never changes is foundational to her spiritual growth.
- Although relationships with peers are becoming more important at this age, parents remain the most important influence in a child's life. Because children are very observant, the example you set will have a great impact on your child. Your child will be watching as you live out what you teach him about God and His truths.

COACHING TIPS

- Because children learn in a variety of ways (visual, reflective, musical, etc.), consider how your child learns best and use those approaches as you teach and reinforce biblical concepts.
- Your child may ask a lot of questions. Instead of always giving an answer, encourage your child to discover the answer by providing him with age-appropriate resources or thought-provoking statements or questions. Work together to discover the biblical truth.
- Every important truth and concept should be grounded in Scripture. Lead your child to understand that what God thinks about something (as stated in the Bible) is always the truth and will never change. Teach (and model) that we are to live our lives based on God's truth, not on what the world around us says or does.

CONVERSATION STARTERS

- **WHAT MIGHT HAVE HAPPENED IF ...** After your child obeys a request you make, evaluate the situation with her. For example, if she goes to bed on time the night before a test instead of staying up late, discuss what might have happened if she hadn't gotten enough sleep. Explain that you set rules because you love her and want the best for her. God does the same for us. Rules and boundaries aren't to punish us but to keep us from making harmful choices. Point out that we should obey God out of our love for Him, just as your child should obey you out of love.
- **I'VE BEEN THINKING ...** As you and your child run errands, discuss ways to tell people about God. Talk about God's love for all people in your community and how you would like your family to find ways to show God's love to them. Encourage suggestions from your child and make plans to follow through with an idea.
- **TELL ME ABOUT ...** Encourage your child to tell you about a project, paper, extracurricular activity, or chore that she has been working on. Ask her about the time spent on it, how much she enjoyed the activity, how she feels the project turned out, and so forth. Remind her that we should always do our best for God, no matter what we are doing.

SAY OR PRAY

- We obey God because we love Him.
- God's truth is the only truth, and it never changes.
- We should find ways to tell other people about God.

BIG IDEA

Raise your preteen with a biblical framework in a confusing culture that attempts to undermine the gospel.

KEY SCRIPTURES

- *We should obey God because we love Him* (John 14:15).
- *We should recognize that God's Word is perfect* (Ps. 18:30; Prov. 30:5-6).
- *We should follow God's will, not that of culture* (Rom. 12:2).
- *We should tell the world why we love and follow Christ* (1 Pet. 3:15).
- *We should not be ashamed of the gospel* (Rom. 1:16).
- *We should set an example for the world* (Titus 2:7-8).

KEY QUESTIONS YOUR PRETEEN MAY ASK

- Are there any mistakes in the Bible? Is it all true?
- How should I talk with my friends about the gospel?
- Why doesn't everyone believe in Jesus?

AT THIS AGE MOST PRETEENS WILL ...

- Begin to adopt a religious belief system of their own.
- Be able to concentrate on things they are interested in.
- Think deeply, quickly, and concretely.
- Memorize information with greater ease.

DEVELOPMENTAL MILESTONES

- Even though preteen boys and girls will feel more independent as they approach puberty, they still have basic physical and emotional needs. These needs include love, trust, acceptance, and security. Meeting these essential needs will make him more receptive to the truths you teach.
- Preteens are generally capable of grasping abstract concepts. They can engage both in literal and figurative thinking. Intentional conversations will become indispensable to reinforce experiences and activities and to direct your preteen toward a more complete gospel framework.
- At the same time your preteen grows out of earlier, imitative phases and exhibits more autonomous behavior, he will still seek approval of peers. Lead by example and talk to your preteen about his stage of growth. Discuss the importance of

friendships but emphasize also the dangers of approval. Be gentle, empathetic, and honest, using your explanations of this milestone to underline the importance of living according to Christ's gospel.

COACHING TIPS

- Explain how you learned about sin and were called to repent and trust in Christ's perfect sacrifice.
- Emphasize that you were saved by grace and not by works. Be ready to share the difference between obedience because of your faith in and love for God as opposed to obeying as a means to earn God's favor.
- Help equip your preteen to live a life modeled on the gospel by highlighting the significance of personal testimony. Speak with your preteen about your own journey as a believer.
- Build and maintain a firm foundation of acceptance and trust to make your preteen more receptive and to keep an open channel of communication. If your preteen trusts you, then he will more readily accept what you say and will feel more comfortable talking to you about difficult topics as he grows.
- Remember to ground every important truth and concept in Scripture. Explain that God's truth is the only truth, and that it will never change. Talking about these truths will help your child shape a gospel-centric worldview in the midst of a relativist culture that glorifies adaptability and alteration.

CONVERSATION STARTERS

- **HOW COULD YOU HAVE DONE THAT DIFFERENTLY?** We all wish for do-overs to fix mistakes, to approach problems differently, or to say something left unspoken. Indeed, we often fail to achieve the standards of a truly gospel-oriented life. This question could help spark new ways for your preteen to reflect on things done or left undone. Be candid and, when appropriate, answer this question yourself.
- **WHO COULD YOU SHARE THE GOSPEL WITH?** Review the importance of love in a gospel-centric life—loving God, loving the church, and loving the unreached. Talk about the need to see people as God sees them and to demonstrate His love to people specifically. Pray for those with whom you need to share the gospel. This will be a powerful example to your child.

SAY OR PRAY

- We obey God because we love Him.
- God's Word is inerrant. It is perfect.
- The gospel truth never changes.
- We love God because He loves us.

BIG IDEA

The gospel should shape the way you parent your middle schooler and should affect every area of your middle schooler's life.

KEY SCRIPTURES

- *Jesus is the only way to salvation* (John 14:6).
- *The Scripture equips us to live for God* (2 Tim. 3:16-17).
- *It is important to be involved with the local church* (Heb. 10:24-25).
- *We should be transformed by God, not conformed to the world* (Rom. 12:1-2).

KEY QUESTIONS YOUR MIDDLE SCHOOLER IS ASKING

- Is Christianity really true? How can I know?
- What does it mean to be a Christian?
- Why does it matter what I believe?

AT THIS AGE MOST MIDDLE SCHOOLERS WILL …

- Have more exposure to other religious beliefs and worldviews.
- Begin to see a connection between one's thinking and one's behavior.
- Begin to connect faith to real life.
- Be excited to be part of the youth ministry.

DEVELOPMENTAL MILESTONES

- Many of the attitudes, beliefs, and values that middle schoolers develop during these years remain with them for life. They move from blindly accepting the convictions of significant adults to developing their own personal values. However, they usually embrace the values of parents or key adults.
- Middle schoolers are usually able to think through ideological topics, argue a position, and challenge adults' thinking and perceptions. Older middle schoolers are able to go deeper than you would expect in a theological discussion about Scripture and the gospel.
- Middle schoolers are eager to learn about topics they find interesting and useful, especially ones that are personally relevant. They like active learning experiences, visual illustrations, and prefer interactions with peers during educational activities. This should shape the way we teach them the Bible.

COACHING TIPS

• Through observation and conversation, assess your middle schooler's relationship with Christ. If she had a salvation experience as a child, watch for fruit of that decision and be prepared to discuss what it really means to follow Jesus. If she's still yet to receive Christ, pray for the Holy Spirit to make her need evident as you clearly present the gospel. Don't pressure her to make this decision, but at the same time, don't procrastinate sharing the gospel.

• Intentionally make connections between biblical truth and everyday life experiences. Help your middle schooler to see his own feelings, words, and actions in light of Scripture.

• Point out the benefits of walking in God's truth: protection from harmful and hurtful consequences of sin, a clean conscience, a good witness to others, and so forth. Remind middle schoolers that God's truth will triumph over false philosophies, ideas, arguments, and religions.

• Guide your middle schooler to understand that she will face opposition as a Christian and to be prepared to stand firm. Pray with your middle schooler about how she can stand firm on the truth of the gospel.

CONVERSATION STARTERS

• **WHAT DOES IT MEAN TO BE A CHRISTIAN?** This will help you gauge where your middle schooler is in his relationship with Jesus. Be an active listener and give him plenty of time to share his thoughts before you begin to share yours.

• **DO YOU HAVE ANY FRIENDS WHO BELIEVE DIFFERENTLY THAN YOU?** This question will help you know the other religious beliefs and worldviews your middle schooler is being exposed to. While you want to make sure your middle schooler knows the truth, be careful not to seem harsh or condemning of his friends.

• **WHAT STORY IN THE BIBLE IS YOUR FAVORITE?** Guide this conversation to talk about the importance of Bible study and growing as a Christian.

SAY OR PRAY

• Pray that your middle schooler will embrace the truth of the gospel. Pray that her life will reflect words, actions, and attitudes that demonstrate Christ.

• Pray with your middle schooler daily about friends and family members who need to know the truth of the gospel. Ask God to provide opportunities for you to share truth with them.

• Encourage your middle schooler to talk about the ways God is working in his life each week.

BIG IDEA

The gospel should shape the way you parent your high schooler and should affect every area of your high schooler's life.

KEY SCRIPTURES

- *Jesus is the only way to salvation* (John 14:6).
- *The Scripture equips us to live for God* (2 Tim. 3:16-17).
- *It is important to be involved with the local church* (Heb. 10:24-25).
- *We should be transformed by God, not conformed to the world* (Rom. 12:1-2).

KEY QUESTIONS YOUR HIGH SCHOOLER IS ASKING

- How do I know Christianity is real?
- Why do I have to go to church?
- Is Jesus really the only way to salvation and heaven?
- Am I truly saved?

AT THIS AGE MOST HIGH SCHOOLERS WILL …

- Have some knowledge of other faiths and religious beliefs and may personally encounter these in friendships and acquaintances.
- Be involved with a number of activities that affects their church attendance.
- Continue to be concerned about being alienated and fitting in.

DEVELOPMENTAL MILESTONES

- Youth at this age will be abstract thinkers, enabling them to wrestle with the doctrines of the faith.
- The change from concrete to abstract thinking may also cause high school students to doubt their personal faith. They may wonder if their childhood decision to follow Christ was authentic.
- At some point during these high school years, most students will obtain their driving licenses. This gives them more freedom to pursue jobs, hobbies, and relationships.
- Some high schoolers are now given the opportunity to choose their level of participation in a local church. Their parents have moved from insisting they go to encouraging their involvement.

COACHING TIPS

- While the student minister and the ministry he or she leads in your church is important to your high schooler's faith development, you are still the primary spiritual developer of your teenager. Continue to have spiritual conversations that challenge your high schooler and hold him accountable.
- If your high schooler was saved at a young age, it's a good possibility she will have doubts about her salvation. Listen closely to what she's saying and evaluate the spiritual fruit of her life. Ask the Holy Spirit to help you discern the truth. Make sure her salvation is based on repentance and faith in the finished work of Christ.
- Don't be hypocritical. Don't let your spiritual instruction be, "Do as I say, not as I do." You are setting the example of what it means to walk with Christ. You don't have to be perfect, but you should be authentic. Keep in mind that rarely will a student rise above the spiritual level of his or her parents.
- These are the last few years to spiritually prepare your child to move out into the world. Make a list of what you want them to know before they leave your home; then be intentional about completing the list.

CONVERSATION STARTERS

- **WHAT DO YOUR FRIENDS THINK ABOUT JESUS?** This will help you assess the spiritual atmosphere in which your high schooler is operating. Also, this question could lead to a conversation about the need for Christians to share our faith with others.
- **IF YOU COULD CHANGE ONE THING ABOUT OUR CHURCH, WHAT WOULD IT BE?** Find out how your high schooler feels about church. Be a good listener. Don't condemn their feelings, and don't jump to defend the church too quickly.
- **WHO IS THE BEST CHRISTIAN YOU KNOW? WHY DID YOU CHOOSE HIM OR HER?** Find out what your student values when it comes to a life of faith.

SAY OR PRAY

- Pray for your high schooler to have a true evaluation of his spiritual condition.
- Pray that your high schooler will be teachable and desire to grow in Christ.
- Encourage your high schooler to share her faith with those who don't know Christ.
- Pray that you would model an authentic Spirit-filled walk with Christ.

BIG IDEA

The gospel should shape the way you parent your young adult and should affect every area of your young adult's life.

KEY SCRIPTURES

- *Jesus is the only way to salvation* (John 14:6).
- *The Scripture equips us to live for God* (2 Tim. 3:16-17).
- *It is important to be involved with the local church* (Heb. 10:24-25).
- *We should be transformed by God, not conformed to the world* (Rom. 12:1-2).

KEY QUESTIONS YOUR YOUNG ADULT IS ASKING

- Is Christianity really true? How can I know?
- Do all religions lead to God?
- Why are my religious beliefs that important?

AT THIS AGE MOST YOUNG ADULTS WILL …

- Encounter other religious beliefs and worldviews through personal relationships and social media.
- Examine and perhaps question the validity of their personal faith.
- Be solidifying their spiritual framework, whether Christian or otherwise.

DEVELOPMENTAL MILESTONES

- Young adults begin to enjoy the freedom they have longed for. Their desire to live independently of their parents is welcomed, but usually without much thought to the responsibilities that accompany that independence.
- Statistics tell us that during this time of life, many young adults will leave the church. Even though they may not totally abandon their faith, they stop attending a local church for various reasons.
- Young adults may go through a crisis of belief as they realize their faith is tied closely to their parents' faith. While this may result in a time of questions and doubts, many young adults emerge from this crisis with a strong personal faith that is their own.
- Relationships with parents and other significant adults remain vitally important to the spiritual well-being of young adults. In fact, they may now have a more open ear to the wisdom of parents than they did in earlier teen years.

COACHING TIPS

- It is important to remember the changing dynamics in your relationship with your young adult. For eighteen-plus years you have parented, for the most part, by insisting. Now, you're suggesting. You're moving from the role of commander to coach.
- Though your role as a parent is changing, you are still in a position to hold your young adult spiritually accountable. Continue to inquire about the state of his walk with the Lord, his involvement in the local church, and the spiritual condition of the people with whom he surrounds himself.
- Don't panic if your young adult goes through a time of questioning her faith. Listen intently and attentively to her struggle. Be patient with her and answer her questions honestly and biblically.
- Perhaps the best spiritual thing you can do for your young adult is intercede for him. He is going to be challenged like never before in all areas of life. Pray continually and specifically for him. Frequently ask him how you can be praying for him and follow through.

CONVERSATION STARTERS

- **WHAT IS THE SPIRITUAL ATMOSPHERE ON YOUR CAMPUS OR AT YOUR WORKPLACE?** After you ask the question, don't be shocked by the answer. This will help you know how to pray for your young adult and the people surrounding her.
- **WHAT OTHER RELIGIONS AND WORLDVIEWS ARE YOU ENCOUNTERING?** This question may assist you in helping your young adult navigate the pluralistic world he is facing.
- **WHO ARE YOUR CLOSEST FRIENDS, AND WHAT ARE THEY LIKE?** Listen with interest, not judgment. Listen in order to pray more specifically. Listen to know who the influencers are in your young adult's life.

SAY OR PRAY

- Pray that your young adult would not conform to this world, but would "be transformed by the renewing of [his] mind" (Rom. 12:2) through the Word of God.
- Pray that your young adult is surrounded by godly people who are speaking truth into her life.
- Pray that the voice of the Holy Spirit is the loudest voice among many in your young adult's life.

SESSION 2

HUMAN DIGNITY

SEEING EVERYONE AS GOD'S IMAGE-BEARERS

Use the space below to record notes, quotes, thoughts, and questions from the video panel discussion.

_____

_____

_____

_____

_____

_____

_____

_____

_____

_____

_____

_____

_____

_____

_____

_____

_____

_____

_____

_____

_____

_____

_____

_____

_____

_____

_____

_____

_____

_____

GROUP GUIDE

Use the following questions and prompts to continue the conversation about the issues discussed by the video panel.

How would you define "dignity"? Do you model a lifestyle that shows you treat everyone with dignity? Explain.

Do you see your children as being fully human? As your neighbor? How does that change your relationships with them?

In your family, how do you highlight and celebrate the differences in people?

How do you help your children stand up for those on the margins of society?

How are you valuing racial diversity in your home? If you're not, how can you?

Is your church working toward racial reconciliation? If so, how is your family taking part? If not, how can your family be a catalyst to move your church in that direction?

If your area/neighborhood is not ethnically diverse, what can you do to create opportunities for your children to do life with those different than them?

What does it mean to value the weak? How can your family do that?

Why is it important for your family to help those who are fostering?

How can your family help those with disabilities and special needs? How does this relate to the sanctity of life and showing dignity to all people?

How are you helping your children respect and value the elderly?

What are some simple things you can do in your family to honor people as made in the image of God?

TAKEAWAYS:

ABORTION AND THE DIGNITY OF THE UNBORN

To diminish human dignity, in any form, is to snuff out the image of God.

IN HIS IMAGE

Every pro-life conversation must begin with an understanding that human beings are created in the image of God—that is, we are created with innate qualities and features that make us like God. By our very nature, human beings "image" or reflect God's likeness back into His creation. This foundational truth has tremendous implications for us both in how we relate to God and how we relate to others.

As image-bearers made in His likeness, we have been given authority to act as His representatives in the world (Gen. 1:26-27). This God-given authority is right and good, but because of sin, it is often misdirected. When God is not in His rightful place on the throne of our hearts, our inclination is to exalt ourselves over others. We begin to believe that some people are more important and more inherently significant than others. This is a fatal error that propagated the institution of slavery and fuels human trafficking.[1] It is the very same lie that says a mother's life is more important than the life she is carrying inside her.

Jesus stands with those the rest of the world deems less than equal. In His kingdom, a person's value does not come from perceived usefulness or apparent worth. It comes from the reality that the image of God is stamped upon every human soul. If we are truly following Christ, we cannot only proclaim the sanctity of human life; we must actively demonstrate our love for the people God has created in His image.[2]

ABORTION IN AMERICA

Sometimes parents are tempted to push off tough conversations about abortion in order to shelter their children from the ugliness of the subject. But if we are to be faithful followers of Jesus, it is critical that we teach our kids about the value of human life and

In God's kingdom, a person's value does not come from perceived usefulness or apparent worth. It comes from the reality that the image of God is stamped upon every human soul.

what it means to stand up for the unborn. Before we look at the Bible's teaching on human dignity, consider for a moment the following information about abortion in America. Nearly half of all pregnancies in the United States are unplanned and about 40 percent of those end in abortion.[3] Between the Supreme Court's 1973 *Roe vs. Wade* decision and 2015, more than fifty-seven million unborn babies were killed in the United States.[4] This is an atrocity. And it is evidence that we have distorted our God-given authority as image-bearers by putting ourselves in the place of God, deciding who should live and who should die.

Logically, we know that if the gestation process is not interrupted, the result is a living, breathing person. Abortion ends this process, which is to say that abortion ends lives. And the truly sad thing is that many people assume the pro-abortion movement has already won on this issue. But even as we recognize that America has in many ways embraced an abortion culture—from a powerful abortion lobby, to the pro-choice messaging coming out of Hollywood, to the subsidizing of abortion providers with public dollars—we also see that there is every reason for hope and optimism.

The pro-life movement has made tremendous strides in recent years. Since the year 2000, young adults aged 18-29 have trended more against abortion than in previous years.[5] Ultrasound technology has

played an outsized role in this shift. Because ultrasounds allow women to see their unborn babies in the womb, mothers now have photos documenting their child's life long before birth. The significance of this is difficult to overstate. Ultrasounds have confronted us with reality. And as a result, more and more people agree that the occupant of a mother's womb is a living human being.

WHAT DOES THE BIBLE SAY?

In Psalm 139, we see God carefully crafting human life:

For it was you who created my inward parts; you knit me together in my mother's womb.
I will praise you because I have been remarkably and wondrously made. Your works are wondrous, and I know this very well. My bones were not hidden from you when I was made in secret, when I was formed in the depths of the earth. Your eyes saw me when I was formless; all my days were written in your book and planned before a single one of them began.
PSALM 139:13-16

The Bible regards the life in the womb with all the significance of a person. God spoke to the prophet Jeremiah saying,

Before I formed you in the womb I knew you.
JEREMIAH 1:5

While we fight desperately to see the end of abortion, we do so proclaiming the hope of the gospel.

And not only did the Son of God spend nine months in the womb of a virgin (Matt. 1:23), but His very presence in Mary's womb caused another child, John the Baptist, to leap with joy while John himself was in the womb of his own mother (Luke 1:41).

Regardless of whether or not your family has been personally affected by the tragedy of abortion, this issue matters because life matters to God. From womb to tomb, every human being bears the image of God, and every one is precious in His sight.

JESUS WAS "THE LEAST OF THESE"

When we minister to an abortion culture, we must speak for the most vulnerable in society. We should cringe when we hear phrases like "medical waste," "fetus," and "products of conception." This demeaning language attempts to lessen the humanity of the unborn and it ought to trigger in us thoughts of Jesus of Nazareth (John 1:14). He was an "embryo." He was a "fetus." He was a nursing infant. He was a child. He is an adult.

As Christians, we should be clear that an attack on vulnerable humanity is an attack on the image of God. That image is not abstract. The image of God has a name and a blood type. The image of God is Christ Jesus Himself, "the firstborn over all creation" (Col. 1:15). Every human image-bearer is patterned after Jesus, the image of the invisible God.

At the cross, Jesus stood with and for humanity in suffering. Jesus was conceived in the most vulnerable situation possible in the ancient world—as a fatherless orphan. He lived as a migrant refugee, His family outrunning King Herod, into a land hostile to His own.

It's an amazing story, that God used a young virgin and a quiet carpenter to preserve the life of the Savior. As parents, we can follow their example of obedience by fighting the spiritual powers that seek to kill, steal, and destroy. We do this by communicating the gospel—of the baby who came to give life—to our children and by teaching them to do the same.[6]

MORE THAN ANTI-ABORTION

Being pro-life means more than being anti-abortion. We cannot only be *against;* we must also be *for.* We must adopt a whole life perspective. We care about the unborn because we care about life. We affirm the dignity of the elderly and infirm, and advocate for compassion and the inclusion of the poor, the orphan, and the widow.

Pure and undefiled religion before God the Father is this: to look after orphans and widows in their distress and to keep oneself unstained from the world.
JAMES 1:27

Teaching your children to value human life is hard. Talking to them about abortion is even more difficult. But there are some simple and practical ways that you can lead your kids toward a whole life, pro-life ethic.

Here is an easy step. Begin by teaching your kids to love children. Encourage them to volunteer in the nursery at church, to babysit for a neighbor, or to help care for little brothers and sisters. Volunteer at a crisis pregnancy center.

Second, teach your children to value human life from its very beginning to its very end. This means caring for orphans, caring for mothers, and caring for the vulnerable. It means we fight human trafficking and sex slavery, and mentor young, at-risk children too.

Third, pray about fostering or adopting children. Far too often we talk about adoption as a last resort for couples with fertility issues. Not only is adoption essential to advancing the pro-life cause, it is at the heart of the gospel we preach.

All of this work must be fueled by utter dependence upon Christ who stands with each of us in our brokenness.

A GOSPEL OF GRACE

Many of those who fall victim to the abortion culture aren't even pro-choice. They are scared and feel they have no other option. There are girls in your own church and neighborhood who are vulnerable because they're afraid of what others will think when their secret is known. And too many times, this fear leads to a tragic mistake—a sorrow-filled trip to the abortion clinic.

As life altering as it may be, your child having an unplanned pregnancy would not be the worst thing that could happen to you. Why? Because there is hope in the gospel of Jesus Christ. He is the Giver of life. He offers forgiveness and mercy.

God is not surprised by our sin. Just as God sees and knows the tiniest human life in the womb, He sees the mother in crisis. He sees the father who is afraid.

While we fight desperately to see the end of abortion, we do so proclaiming the hope of the gospel. Our message is one of forgiveness, love, and restoration. And the offer is good for all who believe (Rom. 1:16). We fight against abortion. We care about the vulnerable. But we always preach hope, even to the moms and dads who will never know their children because of the work of a doctor in a clinic.

QUESTIONS FOR REFLECTION

1. Do you ever stop and think about being an image-bearer of God? How should that truth affect the way we live our lives? How should it affect the way you parent your children?

2. How are you teaching your kids to have a whole-life, pro-life ethic?

3. What are you doing to help your children honor and respect the aged and infirmed?

4. What are some practical things you can do as a family to show love and dignity to those who are marginalized in our society?

5. What one thing stood out to you from this article?

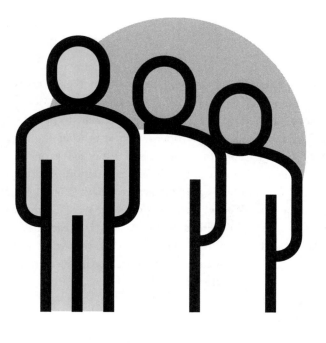

REDEMPTION AND RACIAL RECONCILIATION

We cannot live redemptive lives and hate our neighbor. Diversity in relationships not only shows unity to the world but also builds in our own hearts a love for others.[7]

A NEED FOR RECONCILIATION

In the twenty-first century, our eyes have seen a seemingly endless number of racially-charged acts of violence in America. While it may be tempting to take a passive stance if you are not personally affected, remember that racial reconciliation is a gospel issue. The gospel is a call to reconciliation—first to God and then to others.

Our kids see the ugliness of racism and prejudice every day. As parents, we must be ready to help our children understand and grapple with the complexities of racial issues. There are many reasons to avoid the subject of race when talking to our kids: it is too sensitive, we aren't equipped to respond, or we don't know what to say. But there is a greater danger in keeping quiet. Our silence tells our kids we don't care.

Jesus was in the business of reconciliation. We all—no matter our nationality—were far from Christ and "have been brought near by

[His] blood" (Eph. 2:13). Christ's crucifixion tore down the dividing wall between Jews and Gentiles. In the same way, we are called to be agents of reconciliation (2 Cor. 5:18).

Genuine reconciliation only comes through the peace Christ brings through the gospel. He has freely reconciled us to Himself, and we can follow Him by working toward racial harmony. And just like us, our kids are called to follow Christ as ministers of reconciliation. Are you prepared to equip them?

CELEBRATING DIVERSITY

Let's consider a common obstacle in conversations about race: You are not color-blind, you don't need to be color-blind, and you should strive to not be color-blind. If you'd like to grasp the full beauty of God's creation, see color. Instead of pretending like we are color-blind, let's celebrate God's creation. Ethnic differences aren't the result of the fall; celebrate the unique beauty of each and look forward to seeing heaven filled with the colors of all nations.

Celebrate the diversity (including ethnic distinctions) of those who are called into the family of God. Just like the human body is made of many parts that all need each other, the body of Christ is made of many members working together (1 Cor. 12:12).

Encourage your kids to ask questions about other cultures. Children are often curious when they see people with a different skin color or unique cultural clothing. If they ask questions, don't shame them or make them feel as if they've done something wrong. Help them to see the beauty in our differences.

When those who the world thinks should hate each other instead love each other, the church is testifying that our identity is in Jesus Christ.

RACE AND THE IMAGE OF GOD

How does our understanding of all humanity as God's image-bearers change the way we treat people who are different from us?

As God's image-bearers we are all equal. We are equal in dignity and worth. We are created equally in His image. This is a profound mystery, and yet a great privilege. Understanding our equality as image-bearers changes everything we think about our human relationships.

Everyone we deal with, everyone we come into contact with, is an image-bearer who has intrinsic value. They are not just temporary. They are not an interruption in our day, but rather they are a living, breathing representation of our God. And this is why the subjects of racial reconciliation and kingdom diversity are relevant to all Christians. No one is exempt from recognizing and respecting the image of God in others.

In Ephesians 2:19, Paul declared that those who are in Christ "are no longer foreigners and strangers," but are all "members of God's household." The most important thing about us will never be whether we are white, black, Asian, African, or Hispanic. The most important thing about us is whether or not we belong to Jesus Christ. And if we do, we are all one in His body, brothers and sisters bonded together in love. The family of God

> *In a racially-divided world, the church of Jesus Christ ought not simply advocate for racial reconciliation; we ought to embody it.*

is a diverse family, but we experience unity and harmony because of the work of Christ.

Citizenship in the kingdom of God is not dependent on the color of our skin (Gal. 3:8). Salvation isn't attributed to status, class, or ethnicity. It is a gift offered to all the nations of the world. This is much more than a "black and white" issue. It's about how we respond to the refugees seeking safety in our country. It's about the way we treat the immigrant looking for hope and a future within our borders.

How should we see people? The only answer is to see them as people God loves who are made in His image (Gen 1:26). When the family of God gathers to worship around His throne, every tribe, every language, and every ethnicity will bow down together to offer praises to our King (Rev. 4–5).

We should get comfortable sitting across the table from those who are different from us here on earth, because we will be with all types of people in heaven as part of that "vast multitude from every nation, tribe, people, and language, which no one could number" (Rev. 7:9). And if that is true, then we should pursue it here and now. After all, that is what we pray in the Lord's Prayer:

> Your kingdom come. Your will be done on earth as it is in heaven.
> **MATTHEW 6:10-11a**

RACE AND OUR MISSION

In 1 Corinthians, after Paul's discourse on the body of Christ, he went on to say, if one member of the body suffers, everyone suffers with him (1 Cor. 12:26). Why is race an important issue? Because people have suffered, and continue to suffer. And our silence only serves to intensify the pain. Once our eyes are opened, we sin when we are apathetic toward the work of reconciliation.[8] This isn't an issue for "those people" to deal with. This is an issue for all of God's people.

Reconciliation begins with us and it begins in the church. In a racially-divided world, the church of Jesus Christ ought not simply advocate for racial reconciliation; we ought to embody it. Just as we should speak to the structures of society about principles of morality and righteousness, we also should model those principles in our congregations. The quest for racial unity comes not just through proclamation but through demonstration.

Racial and ethnic division and bigotry are rooted in a satanic deception that tells us we ought to idolize "the flesh." The gospel doesn't just call us individually to repentance, but also congregationalizes that reconciliation in local bodies of persons who may have nothing else in common but the image of God, repentance of sin, and the redemption found in Jesus Christ.

The church, the apostle Paul said, is a sign of God's manifold wisdom, to the principalities and powers in the heavenly places (Eph. 3:10). When God joined together in one church, those who are both Jewish and Gentile, He was doing more than negating the bad effects of ethnic strife. He was declaring spiritual warfare. When those who the world thinks should hate each other instead love each other, the church is testifying that our identity is in Jesus Christ (Col. 3:11). We cannot be pulled apart from each other, because we are one body, and a body that is at war with itself is diseased.

If we begin to see more churches so alive to the gospel that they are not segregated out as "white" or "black" or "Hispanic" or "Asian" or "white collar" or "blue collar," we will start to reflect something of a kingdom of God made up of those "from every tribe and language and people and nation" (Rev. 5:9). And as we know one another as brothers and sisters, we will start to speak up for one another, care for one another, and bear one another's burdens.

We must not merely announce what unity and reconciliation ought to look like. We must also show it. How do we do this? We must first be convinced of the worthiness of the task. Jesus has called us to "make disciples of all nations" (Matt. 28:19). Ask yourself, *Am I willing to subjugate my preferences in obedience to this command?* Second, James's words are also helpful here:

My dear brothers and sisters, understand this: Everyone should be quick to listen, slow to speak, and slow to anger, for human anger does not accomplish God's righteousness.
JAMES 1:19-20

How do you listen to people who are different from you? What steps can you take in your family, in your neighborhood, and in your church to listen and love?

The burden of racial reconciliation is one that every Christian shares. Commit yourself to "the ministry of reconciliation" (2 Cor. 5:18).

A practical place to begin is to invite those different from you into your circle. Welcome a family of a different ethnicity into your home for dinner. Expose your family to other cultures through food and music. Encourage your son or daughter to extend friendship to a child who is new to our country. Host an exchange student for a semester. Pray about international adoption. Model the tangible love of Christ to a diverse world.

The ministry of reconciliation is really about God's love. As we pursue unity amidst diversity, we portray God's love to the world. It is an incredible task, but His grace is sufficient for us. Through the ministry of reconciliation, our God empowers us to be His vehicles of grace in a fallen world.

QUESTIONS FOR REFLECTION

1. How is racial reconciliation a gospel issue?

2. Are you currently having conversations about racial issues in your home? If not, why not?

3. How do you celebrate diversity in your home?

4. What steps will you lead your family to take to practice the ministry of reconciliation?

5. What one thing stood out to you from this article?

DIGNITY AT THE END OF LIFE

Pure and undefiled religion before God the Father is this: to look after orphans and widows in their distress and to keep oneself unstained from the world.
JAMES 1:27

Dealing with death is hard for all of us. It can be especially challenging to approach this issue with our children. Whether it is a beloved grandparent passing away or a friend facing a terminal illness, the reality is that people in our children's lives are going to die. As parents, we need to be prepared to help our kids think about death and human dignity in a biblical way. The way we think about death matters to God, and it should matter to us.

DEATH IS NOT NATURAL

A Christian attitude toward death is shaped by our view of creation. When the apostle Paul spoke of death as an enemy, he did so because he recognized that every funeral wreath echoes an ancient curse: "on the day you eat from it, you will certainly die" (Gen. 2:17). When Jesus wept openly at the death of Lazarus, he did so because death is not natural at all (John 11:35).

American culture is increasingly conflicted about death. On the one hand, the culture treats death as just another medical treatment—embracing abortion, infanticide, suicide, and the euthanasia of the elderly and the sick. On the other hand, American culture is panicked by the thought of death. We idolize youth and beauty, receiving injections to fade our wrinkles and sucking away our midlife pounds with liposuction.

As we advocate for human dignity, we must remember that the root issue here is not ideological or political. The real issue is what the wisdom of God tells us: "All who hate me love death" (Prov. 8:36). That means abortion and euthanasia are part of an ongoing guerrilla insurgency against the image of the Creator Himself.

Christians need to think through what it means to follow a resurrected Messiah. The very Word of God took on our humanity so that "through his death he might destroy the one holding the power of death—that is, the devil—and free those who were held in slavery all their lives by the fear of death" (Heb. 2:14b-15). We need to stop trying to domesticate death. We need to learn to view it the way Jesus Himself does—as an enemy to be destroyed.

We need to learn to hate death. That will take a worldview shift for some of us. We sing songs about death as "some glad morning" and speak of a funeral as a happy "graduation day" for the believer. We know that Scripture says "to die is gain" but we forget that it also says that "to live is Christ" (Phil. 1:21). Our hope is not in death itself, but in the pioneer who has passed through the jaws of death—and will raise us with Him, never again to die.

A FUNDAMENTAL JUSTICE ISSUE

More than 20 times, the Bible gives instructions for the care of widows—often coupled with caring for orphans.

You must not mistreat any widow or fatherless child. If you do mistreat them, they will no doubt cry to me, and I will certainly hear their cry.
EXODUS 22:22-23

God in his holy dwelling is a father of the fatherless and a champion of widows.
PSALM 68:5

Learn to do good; seek justice, correct oppression; bring justice to the fatherless, plead the widow's cause.
ISAIAH 1:17

This is a fundamental justice issue that cannot be overlooked. Every family has someone who is aging. Every aging generation is looking to a younger generation to care for them. Sometimes this will mean making space for a loved one in your home. It might mean providing financially for medical needs like ongoing in-home care. When we care for the elderly

in this way we model love and justice for our kids (1 Tim. 5:4).

You may have questions about medical care for those in the final stages of life. As a starting point, treat them as people worthy of dignity and honor their person-hood. When someone is beyond the point of recovery and death is imminent, provide comfort care. It is right to provide care even when treatment is no longer a good option. Make the final stages of life as dignified as possible for the dying.

Death provides us a precious opportunity to share the gospel. When a loved one dies, help your children learn from both the encouraging and complicated aspects of that person's life. Tell your kids about the hope of eternal life in Jesus Christ who died once and for all so that all may live. Proceed with caution if the family member wasn't a believer. Our hope is juxtaposed with the crushing reality that some will spend eternity separated from Christ. Help your kids understand the lingering curse of death in our world and communicate the urgency of the gospel message (Jas. 4:14).

The cross says that no one is hopeless. This is the message we must lead our children to believe and embrace.

A SLIPPERY SLOPE

Do we have the right to decide when someone should die? The answer is no. God is the giver and sustainer of life (Acts 17:25). A Christian perspective on death will stand in stark contrast to the views of culture. If Jesus is "the life" (John 14:6), then issues of life and death are ultimately gospel issues.

One area that we should give attention to is the growing acceptance of assisted suicide. This is not merely another skirmish in the "culture war." It is an expression of one of the biggest religious alternatives to historic, orthodox Christianity in our world today—death itself.

The well-crafted arguments in favor of ending life for the ill, paralyzed, and now the depressed and bored depend on the idea that death is just a natural part of life. If one cannot bear the burden of an immobile body, an unwanted child, or an unresponsive spouse, you can just ease the transition from consciousness to annihilation. That's not just a political position. It is a religion. But it is a religion that denies what God has said is true about humanity.

Practices like physician-assisted suicide provide people the ability to end their own lives in a so-called dignified manner. Proponents of physician-assisted suicide (and euthanasia) argue that their methods are compassionate. They are easing a person's pain and relieving surviving family members of the burdensome cost of medical care. They argue that once a person is in such a physical or mental state that they have no possibility of recovery then it is actually more ethical to end life than to sustain it.

On the surface, it sounds noble. Wouldn't it be compassionate to ease someone's suffering at the end of life and make the transition into eternity more comfortable? If a person is in pain, wouldn't it be simpler to let them die?

Hopefully you can see the obvious flaw in this line of reasoning. But it is even more unconvincing once we look at the history of this issue and see the slippery slope ahead.

Initial legislation for these practices in Western Europe allowed for physician-assisted suicide in extreme cases when suffering was beyond what the patient was able to bear. However, both legislation and the feeling of the general population have evolved to include those who are depressed or simply tired of living. Between 2010 and 2013, the number of euthanasia cases in Belgium doubled, and more than ten percent of these were patients who were not facing imminent death.[9] The practice is gaining popularity in North America as well. As of 2015, physician-assisted suicide was legal in five states, while nine more had pending legislation.[10] Where does it end?

Assisted suicide is dangerous because, rather than preserving, it undermines human dignity. It denies the inherent value of life and it locates our will in the place of

God's purpose and plan. Christians are not pragmatists. We must not defend things like assisted suicide out of convenience or sentimentality.

And this says nothing about actual suicide. While past generations have regarded the practice of suicide as shameful and tragic, the culture of death is inching closer to acknowledging suicide as an acceptable practice.

Suicide is the deliberate destruction of the image of God. And like abortion, it is based on a lie. People commit suicide because they are convinced they have no value and they feel they have no hope. The gospel speaks a better word than this. God says that all who bear His image have intrinsic value and inherent dignity. The cross says that no one is hopeless. This is the message we must lead our children to believe and embrace.

LOVING THE LEAST OF THESE

The implications of this conversation reach far beyond our loved ones near the end of life on earth. When we value life, we must treat all people with dignity and grace. This means we embrace children and adults with special needs and minister to those who have no other functioning capacity but the breath that God put in their lungs. They have worth in the kingdom of God.

As we encounter questions about death, let us endeavor to treat people made in God's image with dignity and respect, regardless of gender, race, age, nationality or economic status. Remember our King's words:

Whatever you did for one of the least of these brothers and sisters of mine, you did for me.
MATTHEW 25:40

Above all, our goal is to honor God. We can do this by teaching our children to respect His image. We truly want them to be whole life, pro-life people who are prepared to deal with the complexities of issues like abortion, race, and death in light of the gospel.

QUESTIONS FOR REFLECTION

1. What are your personal feelings about death?

2. Have you had discussions about death with your children? If so, evaluate how you handled it. If not, how will you deal with it?

3. When it comes to caring for the aging, is that something you embrace or shun? Explain.

4. How are you teaching and modeling for your children loving and caring for "the least of these"?

5. What one thing stood out to you from this article?

BIG IDEA

Help your child develop a reverence for life as created in the image of God in a society filled with threats to the sanctity of life.

KEY SCRIPTURES

- *All people are fearfully and wonderfully made* (Ps. 139:13-14).
- *All people are made in God's image* (Gen. 1:27).
- *God cares for all people* (Ps. 145:9).
- *All life is important* (Ex. 20:13).
- *All people are planned by God before they are born* (Jer. 1:5).

KEY QUESTIONS YOUR PRESCHOOLER IS ASKING

- Does God love all people the same?
- Why should I care about people who are different from me?
- How does God plan for children to grow?

AT THIS AGE MOST PRESCHOOLERS WILL …

- Gradually begin to understand the concept of time.
- Explore relationships outside of the family.
- Begin to understand basic abstract ideas.

DEVELOPMENTAL MILESTONES

- Preschoolers mostly understand the concept of growing, with thoughts like, *Babies will someday grow to be as big as me.* Pointing out connections between pregnancy, babies, children, adults, and seniors can further their understanding of life development.
- Children at this age are extremely self-focused, so directing their attention to others' feelings or thoughts can encourage compassion and understanding from an early age.
- As a parent, you are your child's primary example of how to act. Model empathy as often as possible, and talk with your child about caring for others. Praise others often, and be generous with compliments or support.
- Reinforcing good behavior is an effective way to mold behavior and character, so recognize and commend any display of kindness to others. However, be sure not to over-praise him, or the attention may become his primary motivation for kindness.

- Preschoolers do not yet understand the finality of death, as they will likely view it as reversible or impersonal. Use concrete or familiar examples to help them understand. Every child responds to the subject differently.

COACHING TIPS

- Teach your children how a baby develops from being so small we can't see it to growing up to be an adult. Showing photos of an ultrasound or discussing an unborn baby's development can help solidify the concept of life stages for your child.
- Make it a point to recognize and celebrate other cultures and races. Be open about discussing cultural differences, but be sure to emphasize that others' differences do not change how God feels about them. God loves all people.
- In explaining death, while saying someone is "with God now" or "in heaven with the angels" might be comforting to adults, it might confuse preschoolers when they still see the sadness of others. Give simple and short answers to your child's questions, but reassure her about her worries. Try to avoid common euphemisms for death, such as "resting," "sleep," or "gone away," as this could incite fear of sleep or separation in your child.

CONVERSATION STARTERS

- **LET'S SING A SONG.** Common children's songs, like "Jesus Loves Me" or "He's Got the Whole World in His Hands," can provide points of discussion as you explore God's love for all people and all life.
- **WHO DO YOU LOOK LIKE?** Using a mirror or photographs, begin a discussion on image and mention how children often look like their parents. Segue into a conversation about humans being made in God's image. Our lives are valuable because God made us in His image, and each person is uniquely important.
- **LET'S GO HELP OTHERS.** Find a volunteer activity to do with your child that serves others, whether in a soup kitchen for the homeless or spending time at a nursing home. When your child connects with different kinds of people, he develops a value for people of all stages or situations in life, and he learns that everyone is unique and valuable.

SAY OR PRAY

- God created you.
- God created life, and all life comes from God.
- God created everyone differently, but He loves them the same.
- God created you to show His love to others.

BIG IDEA

Help your child develop a reverence for life as created in the image of God in a society filled with threats to the sanctity of life.

KEY SCRIPTURES

- *All people are fearfully and wonderfully made* (Ps. 139:13-14).
- *All people are made in God's image* (Gen. 1:27).
- *God cares for all people* (Ps. 145:9).
- *All life is important* (Ex. 20:13).
- *All people are planned by God before they are born* (Jer. 1:5).

KEY QUESTIONS YOUR ELEMENTARY-AGED CHILD IS ASKING

- What does it mean to be created in the image of God?
- Are some lives more important than others?
- What happens when people die?

AT THIS AGE MOST ELEMENTARY CHILDREN WILL …

- Begin to show empathy and offer help when they see someone in need.
- Value their friendships more and may desire to be popular.
- Begin to develop a conscience and a value system.
- Be interested in their own community and country.

DEVELOPMENTAL MILESTONES

- Children at this age are becoming more sensitive to the feelings of others. They begin to imagine how it would feel to be in someone else's situation. They may desire to help others. Model empathy and caring for other people. Compliment your child when you observe her helping others who are in need.
- Younger elementary age kids often develop a strong sense of right and wrong (moral sense). They may begin to express opinions about fairness and making the world a better place. Be willing to engage in conversation with your child about his thoughts and feelings on topics relating to human dignity.
- Most younger elementary age children understand the finality of death, but some may have difficulty grasping why God allowed a person to die or what happens to a person after death. When questions arise, provide answers, avoiding abstract terms like "sleeping," "resting," and so forth.

COACHING TIPS

- Because people are God's most important creation, encourage your child to begin seeing—and treating—every person as God's creation: loved and valued by Him. When we do this, we please God and honor Him.
- God works through people who do His work in their communities and in the world. Lead your family to reach out to people of other races, cultures, ages, socio-economic situations, special needs, and so forth, to champion human dignity and for the glory of God.
- God has a plan and purpose for every person's life. Help your child learn to trust that God's plan is always best, even when things happen that don't make sense (like death, poverty, sickness, etc.).

CONVERSATION STARTERS

- **LOOK AT THESE PEOPLE!** Look through several magazines with your child, comparing the different types of people pictured throughout the pages. Talk about the ways people are different. Emphasize that God values every person, and we should value all people, too. Invite your child to name some ways to value other people.
- **LET'S LOOK AT YOUR BABY PICTURES.** Invite your child to look at her baby pictures with you. Note the many ways she has changed and grown. Transition into a discussion about people being created in God's image and how each of us is important and has a purpose.
- **WHAT CAN WE DO?** Look for volunteer opportunities at places such as nursing homes or homeless shelters where you and your child can spend time serving others together. As your child connects with people of other cultures, races, and stages in life, he will understand their importance as God's creations. Volunteering will help him develop a sense of value for each person.

SAY OR PRAY

- People are God's most important creation.
- God created us in His image.
- God loves and values every person.
- God has a plan for every person's life.

BIG IDEA

Help your preteen develop a reverence for life as created in the image of God in a society filled with threats to the sanctity of life.

KEY SCRIPTURES

- *All people are made in God's image* (Gen. 1:27).
- *You shall not murder* (Ex. 20:13).
- *God designed all people. He knew our futures before we were born* (Ps. 139:13-16).
- *You should value your elders* (Prov. 23:22).
- *God alone should determine life and death* (Job 14:5).
- *All people are equally valuable in the eyes of God* (Job 31:15).

KEY QUESTIONS YOUR PRETEEN MAY ASK

- Why do people treat certain people differently?
- How should I act toward everyone?
- Is every life equal?
- How should I relate to people who don't share my views?

AT THIS AGE MOST PRETEENS WILL ...

- Begin to develop a conscience, a value system, and concepts of love and trust.
- Have formed concepts of personal worth.
- Feel deeply about their own experiences and can be sensitive to others.

DEVELOPMENTAL MILESTONES

- Preteens experience rapid social and emotional growth. Although they may begin this life stage motivated by their own interests and experiences, they generally exhibit a newfound eagerness for responsibilities and opportunities for self-direction.
- Abstract thinking gives way to an ability to distinguish between fact and fiction, as well as the capacity for discerning relationships in terms of time and space.
- Preteens understand the finality of death but are easily influenced by their emotions and emotional reflexes. Use Scripture to help guide them to a healthy understanding of life and death. Apply personal experience gently to reinforce, in a balanced emotional approach to life, its fragility and its ultimate sanctity.
- Many preteens will be aware of the processes underlying life development and may ask practical, moral, and/or political questions about its contingent or theoretic value. Ground your responses in Scripture.

• As a parent, you are your preteen's primary example of how to act. Model empathy as often as possible and talk with your preteen about caring for others. Praise other people often and be generous with compliments and support.

COACHING TIPS

• Discuss how all people develop according to the same process from infancy to adulthood to solidify the concept of life stages. Use Scripture to point out how biblical persons were just as human as yourself and your preteen, and how amazing works of God are done through people who are subject to the same process of physical growth. All human life, therefore, is sacred, God-given, and must be treated with utmost respect.

• Recognize and celebrate other cultures and races. Clarify how the differences between cultures, people groups, and accompanying modes of expression *do not* alter God's love for all people. Watch movies or read books together that take on cultural issues appropriately to provide her with a healthy venue for understanding challenging or complicated issues. Discuss the Civil Rights Movement and why we should show love and respect to all people. Explain that we can love the way Jesus loved and remain true to what the Bible says is true, even though it may be difficult and not always received well by others.

• While preteens are more capable of grasping the concept of death than younger children, be attuned to your preteen's emotions as well as his holistic understanding. Be reassuring but assertive in your coaching, reminding him of God's promise of eternal life for believers after death.

CONVERSATION STARTERS

• **LET'S GO HELP OTHERS.** Engage in a volunteer organization, program, or activity with your preteen. Work together to serve others. Your preteen will develop a love for people, no matter her stage or situation in life. Outreach will help reinforce in your preteen how everyone is unique and valuable.

• **WHAT HAVE YOU HEARD ON THE NEWS OR FROM FRIENDS ABOUT THE MEANING OF LIFE, DEATH, AND WHEN LIFE BEGINS?** Encourage your preteen to share while you listen attentively. Treat these conversations as opportunities to grow closer together over tough subjects. Teach your preteen that studying the Bible deeply is a crucial step toward disentangling some of life's most troubling issues.

SAY OR PRAY

• God created life, and all life comes from God.
• God designed everyone differently, but He loves each person the same.
• God wants to have a relationship with you.
• God made you to show His love to others.

BIG IDEA

Your middle schooler needs to know that every human life, regardless of age or ability, has inherent value from being created in God's image.

KEY SCRIPTURES

- *Every person is created in God's image* (Gen. 1:26-27).
- *Every person created in God's image has inherent value, dignity, and worth* (Ps. 139:13,16; Jer. 1:5).
- *We are to love all people regardless of their situation or who they are* (Mark 12:28-31).
- *Taking innocent life created in God's image is sinful* (Gen. 9:5-6).

KEY QUESTIONS YOUR MIDDLE SCHOOLER IS ASKING

- Why am I supposed to love everyone?
- What does it mean to be made in the image of God?
- Why can't we get along with everyone?
- Why would someone want to kill their baby?

AT THIS AGE MOST MIDDLE SCHOOLERS WILL …

- Begin to develop an opinion on the sanctity of human life.
- Begin to engage with the arguments coming from both sides of the issue, at least those presented in pop culture and their friends.
- Recognize injustice and bias in the adults and peers around them. They often will have strong reactions to those being unfairly judged or those treated unfairly.

DEVELOPMENTAL MILESTONES

- Middle schoolers will see and some will experience bullying including racial slurs and acts of aggression toward someone. Create a listening environment for them to talk through what they see, hear, and how they feel.
- During middle school there is a link between self-worth or self-hatred and rebellious behavior. Middle schoolers need to be treated with dignity and respect, kindness and firm discipline.
- Most middle schoolers want to explore moral and ethical issues confronted in the culture, media, and daily interactions they experience in their families and with peer groups.

COACHING TIPS

- Genesis 1 shows that every person is made in God's image. We are God's image-bearers with value and worth because we reflect Him. Think about ways you can instill this value in your middle schooler on a consistent basis through your words, actions, responses, and attitude. Make sure you are treating your middle schooler in this way.
- David declares that the Lord "knit me together in my mother's womb" (Ps. 139:13). Help your middle schooler understand that this is true of every person whether they know Christ or not. Discuss how as a family you can demonstrate your understanding that all life is sacred—even with unbelievers.
- The Scriptures clearly teach that humans are made in God's image and therefore have innate value. Discuss how as a family you've messed up and stereotyped people or failed to show that others were of great value. Don't be afraid to own your mistakes and change. Discuss what you can do differently.
- Provide opportunities for your middle schooler to interact with people who are different than her. Plan family activities that make this happen, including having people of different races and ethnicities in your home. You may need to move out of your own comfort zone to accomplish this.
- Be an example of what you are teaching. It will be hard to teach your middle schooler to love and respect all people if you are not setting that example.

CONVERSATION STARTERS

- **WHO ARE SOME OF YOUR FRIENDS WHO ARE DIFFERENT THAN YOU?** Push your middle schooler to think beyond superficial differences and think about those different racially, ethnically, economically, and so forth. If she struggles to name anyone, that's a good clue you need to provide opportunities for her to meet some new friends.
- **WHAT DOES IT MEAN TO BE CREATED IN GOD'S IMAGE?** Let your middle schooler wrestle with this question. He's probably heard the phrase but may not have really thought about what it means.
- **HAVE YOU EVER HEARD OR SEEN SOMEONE EXPRESS RACISM?** If your middle schooler answers negatively, talk about what her response would be if a friend made a racist joke or made a racist statement.

SAY OR PRAY

- Pray that God would give you and your middle schooler the courage to take a stand for the inherent value, dignity, and worth of each person created in the image of God.
- Pray your middle schooler would have a heart for people not like him.

BIG IDEA

Your high schooler needs to know that every human life, regardless of age or ability, has inherent value from being created in God's image.

KEY SCRIPTURES

- *Every person is created in God's image* (Gen. 1:26-27).
- *Every person created in God's image has inherent value, dignity, and worth* (Ps. 139:13,16; Jer. 1:5).
- *We are to love all people regardless of their situation or who they are* (Mark 12:28-31).
- *Taking innocent life created in God's image is sinful* (Gen. 9:5-6).

KEY QUESTIONS YOUR HIGH SCHOOLER IS ASKING

- What does it mean to be made in the image of God?
- Why is there so much racial tension in our world?
- How do I treat people who are different than me?
- Is it ever OK for someone to have an abortion?

AT THIS AGE MOST HIGH SCHOOLERS WILL ...

- Increasingly encounter people different than them—racially, economically, religiously, and so forth.
- Be greatly influenced by their peer group on how they are supposed to think about and treat others.
- Be forming opinions on sanctity of life issues.

DEVELOPMENTAL MILESTONES

- High schoolers will become more aware of the differences in people and will be more open to developing relationships with them.
- Youth at this age will begin to become less self-focused and begin expressing empathy toward others, especially those in need. Many will be moved by the situations of the oppressed in the world and become interested in social causes.
- High schoolers will have a deeper capacity for caring, sharing, and developing more intimate relationships.
- Youth at this age are engaged in higher-level thinking and abstract problem solving, which means they may want to ask and wrestle with tough questions about abortion and other sanctity of life issues.

COACHING TIPS

- It's difficult to respect and care for people different than you if you don't know or aren't around people of varying races, cultures, or statuses. Provide opportunities for your high schooler to interact with people different than them. You may have to push her a bit to get her outside of her comfort zone. But first, you must be willing to move outside your own comfort zone to make this happen.
- Your high school student may show lots of concern, care, and respect for people in difficult situations around the world, while showing little of that for you and the rest of the family. Remind her that showing people honor and dignity begins at home.
- Treat your high schooler with respect and dignity. It's difficult to ask him to do this for others if you are not loving him in this way.
- Be willing to have conversations with your high schooler about difficult sanctity of life issues, and do so from a biblical perspective. She will have plenty of voices speaking the secular view. Make sure she understands how the gospel shapes our view of all people.
- Talk about how Christ treated us when we were His enemies: He chose to die for us (Rom. 5:8).

CONVERSATION STARTERS

- **WHAT DO YOU THINK IT MEANS TO BE MADE IN THE IMAGE OF GOD?** High schoolers are definitely not too young to be tackling this question. Follow this question by discussing how the truth that we are all image-bearers of God should shape the way we see and treat people.
- **WHAT WOULD YOU DO TO QUIET THE RACIAL TENSION IN OUR COMMUNITY AND COUNTRY?** Talk about how you and your family can be instruments of peace in this area.
- **WHAT WOULD YOU SAY TO A FRIEND WHO WAS CONSIDERING ABORTING HER BABY?** This question will open doors to talk about this difficult issue. You may find that what she nods her assent to in church is different from what she really feels about the issue.

SAY OR PRAY

- Pray that your high schooler will see himself and others as made in the image of God.
- Pray that you and your family will be instruments of peace and messengers of reconciliation in a world of conflict and lostness.
- Repent of your own prejudices and pray that you would model for your high schooler how to truly love others as Christ loves them.

BIG IDEA

Your young adult needs to know that every human life, regardless of age or ability, has inherent value from being created in God's image.

KEY SCRIPTURES

- *Every person is created in God's image* (Gen. 1:26-27).
- *Every person created in God's image has inherent value, dignity, and worth* (Ps. 139:13,16; Jer. 1:5).
- *We are to love all people regardless of their situation or who they are* (Mark 12:28-31).
- *Taking innocent life created in God's image is sinful* (Gen. 9:5-6).

KEY QUESTIONS YOUR YOUNG ADULT IS ASKING

- What does it mean to be created in the image of God?
- Why is there so much racial division in our country?
- Why is abortion wrong?

AT THIS AGE MOST YOUNG ADULTS WILL …

- Likely be in an environment where they consistently encounter various cultures, races, and ethnicities.
- Be engaging in experiences, conversations, and situations where sanctity of life is a prominent issue.
- Probably know someone who has had or is contemplating having an abortion.

DEVELOPMENTAL MILESTONES

- Young adults are experiencing significant changes in their ability to think. They are able to wrestle with complex abstract ideas and do future thinking. They also are more capable of empathy toward others. This will affect the way they view the sanctity of life issue.
- At this age, young adults are able to consider different points of view, which enables them to have more concern for those around them. They may struggle at times balancing concern for others with the truth.
- Young adults will begin to formulate strong opinions concerning sanctity of life and human dignity issues. They may feel strongly about human injustices and want to find ways to take action.
- Because young adults' environment is more culturally diverse, their friend group is likely to reflect that environment, which could include friends of different races, ethnicities, faith, and sexual orientation.

COACHING TIPS

- Remind your young adult that all people are made in the image of God and have worth and value because of that. You may get that opportunity in a conversation about a professor he doesn't like, a drill sergeant who's pushing him hard, or a boss he doesn't respect.
- When discussing a controversial subject, seek to have a reasoned conversation that ends well, even if the two of you don't agree. This could help teach your young adult the art of agreeing to disagree. You want to make sure to leave the door open for further conversations about the subject.
- Talk about how Christ treated us when we were His enemies: He chose to die for us (Rom. 5:8).
- It's going to be very difficult to have respectful conversation about human dignity if you don't see and treat your young adult as an adult. In a conversation, show her the same respect you would other adults, even if you disagree.
- Be prepared for your young adult to express strong opinions that are different than yours. It could be that he doesn't yet hold that position but is outwardly processing it.

CONVERSATION STARTERS

- **DO YOU THINK ALL PEOPLE HAVE VALUE? WHY OR WHY NOT?** This question could easily lead into a discussion about what it means to be made in the image of God.
- **DO YOU SENSE RACIAL TENSION IN YOUR DORM/AT YOUR WORKPLACE/IN YOUR MILITARY UNIT?** You may be a safe place for your young adult to discuss this subject. This may also give you an opportunity to help her explore how God could use her to be an instrument of peace in the situation.
- **WHO ARE SOME SENIOR ADULTS YOU ADMIRE? WHY DID YOU CHOOSE THEM?** Use this question to remind your young adult that our elders still have value and so much to give. This conversation could lead to discussing ways to love and minister to the senior adults around you.

SAY OR PRAY

- Pray that your young adult would have the courage to take a stand for the inherent value, dignity, and worth of each person created in the image of God.
- Pray that your young adult will be sensitive to those who may be struggling with life decisions that have huge implications, such as whether or not to have an abortion.
- Ask God to constantly remind your young adult that he has value because he is an image-bearer of the Creator. Sometimes it's easy to remember that for someone else but forget it for yourself.

SESSION 3

IDENTITY

ANSWERING THE QUESTION OF "WHO AM I?"

Use the space below to record notes, quotes, thoughts, and questions from the video panel discussion.

_____

_____

_____

_____

_____

_____

_____

_____

_____

_____

_____

_____

_____

_____

_____

_____

_____

_____

_____

_____

_____

_____

_____

_____

_____

_____

_____

_____

_____

_____

_____

_____

_____

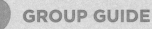

Use the following questions and prompts to continue the conversation about the issues discussed by the video panel.

What cultural pressures are you seeing in the area of identity? How is this affecting your children?

Why is gender identity such a big issue in the teen years? How can you help your teenager deal with this?

What are some wrong things parents pressure their children to find their identity in? Have you been guilty of this? Explain.

How have you seen parents push their children too hard? What do you think was the reason? How have you applied too much pressure to your child?

Are you currently trying to help your child live up to God's potential or your vision? Explain.

How can you affirm the way the Lord has created your child?

Are you comfortable allowing your child to be who he or she is? Explain.

David Prince said most of us are role players in life. What do you think he meant? Do you agree? How do we communicate that in a healthy way?

Do you ever struggle to tell your child the truth? Explain.

How are you currently teaching and reflecting biblical manhood and womanhood in your home? How do you do this without reverting to stereotypes?

If your child were in crisis, who would you turn to for help? Why is it important for your child to have other godly influences in his or her life?

How are you currently affirming and celebrating your child's gender and rejecting the stereotypes and confusion?

TAKEAWAYS:

A CHRIST-CENTERED IDENTITY

God created little images so that they would talk and act and feel in a way that reveals the way God is.[1]

SONS AND DAUGHTERS

Sooner or later every child will ask, *Who am I?* Parenting is an incredible stewardship from the Lord and one of its greatest privileges is having the opportunity to shape the way our kids see themselves and the world around them. More than anything else, we want our children to understand who they are in light of Whose they are. We want our kids to ground their identities in their status as sons and daughters of God, which means they must see themselves through the lens of the gospel.

Here are three keys for parents who want to instill a gospel-shaped identity in their child.

A LOVE TO EXPERIENCE

In our homes, we must model the love of a heavenly Father who showed His love for us while we were still sinners by sending Christ to die for us (Rom. 5:8). Of course, our kids can and will disappoint us at times, but our homes are supposed to be a living picture of the gospel. We are sinners, but nothing "will be able to separate us from the love of God" (Rom. 8:39). This is why we go out of our way to show our kids that we love them because of who they are, not because of what they do. Our love teaches them about God's love.

If your child is going to embrace his or her true identity, it will be the result of a deeply-embedded belief that God's love is not conditional. They will learn this from you. So teach your kids right from wrong and exercise loving discipline, but never let them lose sight of your unconditional love toward them. Our end-goal with each of our kids is for them to become faithful followers of Jesus, who live in light of His calling and purpose, and to experience their true identity, which is firmly established in Him.

We can model our parenting after the Fatherhood of God. God disciplines and trains us up for life in the future He has waiting for us. This isn't a sign that we are out of His favor but a sign that He loves us and has a plan for our lives (Heb. 12:3-11). God does not give us everything we want in our immaturity. That's

If your child is going to embrace his or her true identity, it will be the result of a deeply-embedded belief that God's love is not conditional.

not because He is hostile to us; it's because God is training us up to be heirs (Gal. 4:1-7).

As parents, we will never get this completely right. Unlike the Father, we are not all-holy, and we are not all-knowing. We will stumble in many ways, and we are sometimes unable to see exactly what steps are in our child's best interest in the long-term. But even so, we are much better equipped to guide them than they are to guide themselves.

This brings us back to love and identity. Raising kids to embrace a Christ-centered identity means we must parent from a Christ-centered identity. As we throw all our faith and trust on the One who makes us complete in Him and supplies all our needs (Phil. 4:19), we do the hard work of pointing our kids to Jesus in the ways that we love and parent them.

A PLACE TO BELONG

Just as all of our kids will one day ask, *Who am I?*, all of our kids will eventually begin to seek out community. Humans are relational beings. God made us that way, because He made us like Him. Our deep desire for relationships is patterned after the perfect relationships enjoyed by the members of the Trinity. Community is a powerful, God-given force in our lives.

Grasping the significance of community is especially important for parents. A person's community plays an outsize role in shaping his or her identity. As they grow up, our children will seek a place of belonging. Part of figuring out who they are is finding out where they fit in.

Fortunately, most of you are already intimately familiar with God's answer to this longing. God has established the local church to be the natural gathering point for His people. One of the most important things you can do for your kids is make sure they are connected to God's people in a healthy and faithful local church. If your children find community in the church, this will inevitably point them to one of the most fundamental truths about a Christian's identity: in addition to being loved by God, we are all part of one body with many members (1 Cor. 12:12).

This will provide a desperately needed counterbalance to the message the culture is preaching. The world invites our kids to embrace a narcissistic, self-focused mentality that screams "everything is about me." Through the gospel and the church, we can help our kids embrace an accurate view of themselves. One that rightly estimates their inherent value and dignity, but balances this reality by locating the rightful place of the individual as a son or daughter in the family of God.

All of this, again, points us to Jesus. Though He had every right to elevate Himself,

He humbled himself by becoming obedient to the point of death—even to death on a cross.
PHILIPPIANS 2:8

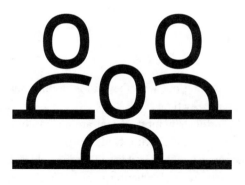

Like love and belonging, the culture has hijacked purpose and turned it inward.

Our culture says, "Believe in yourself" and Jesus says, "Deny yourself and follow me." No one can do both ... An entitlement mentality is at odds with the gospel message and God's promise; it is "through many tribulations we must enter the Kingdom of God" (Acts 14:22).[2]
DAVID PRINCE

God's only begotten Son gave His "life as a ransom for many" (Matt. 20:28). And you are to lead your kids to follow Jesus by considering "others as more important than yourselves" (Phil. 2:3). Jesus loves us individually, but He calls us to give up our lives for the sake of one another. This is a radically counter-cultural message, and it is the essence of Christian community.

Help your kids understand how they belong in relationship to God and how they belong in relationship to others. Make no mistake, your kids will find community. And while we often hear the words "peer pressure" carelessly tossed into conversations about parenting, remember that community fosters identity. It matters a great deal who has influence over your kids. Make every effort to help your kids find their place among the people of God, where their faith will be nurtured and their identity will be shaped by the gospel.

A PURPOSE TO PURSUE

We have seen that love and community will shape a child's identity. The final key for parents is to help your children cultivate a sense of purpose.

The point of discovering our purpose is not to lift up self but to lift up Christ. In its most basic form, that *is* our purpose: we are citizens of the kingdom seeking to exalt the King. Leading your kids to recognize their purpose—to live out the mission God has given us—will be truly liberating for them. As they live their lives to glorify God and to make Him known, they will not be driven by performance but by obedience. Of course we want to encourage them to hone and develop their talents and special abilities, but we encourage them to do so in order to glorify Jesus and serve others, not themselves.

The beautiful thing about grounding your identity in the gospel is that it produces so much freedom. If our children believe they are valuable because God loves them, then they will be free to work, free to fail, free to serve, and free to rest. They can confidently pursue whatever God-honoring opportunity, gifting, or talent they desire because they rely upon having God's approval instead of the approval of others. And best of all, no matter what kind of obstacles they encounter or setbacks they endure, they can persevere in their kingdom-driven obedience through

Make every effort to help your kids find their place among the people of God, where their faith will be nurtured and their identity will be shaped by the gospel.

the Holy Spirit (Rom. 5:3-5).

We can attempt all of these things because we know that no amount of earthly accomplishments will impress God. Our status in Him is based on grace alone through Christ's substitutionary death on the cross that brought us peace with God and established us as sons and daughters of the King (Eph. 2:8-10). Whatever gifts we have, they came from Him (1 Cor. 4:7). Imagine how your kids might prosper if they embrace this truth.

PUT IT TO PRACTICE

We put this conversation in proper perspective by seeing ourselves in relation to the Almighty God. We are finite; He is infinite. We are limited in knowledge; He is all-knowing. When we consider the greatness of God, we understand our place in His world. The God of the universe knows us intimately. He has counted "the hairs of your head" (Luke 12:7). And that is why we matter.

When your daughter feels unimportant or unwanted, remind her that she is a special creation formed by a loving God and made in His image. He sees her, He knows her, and

He has a plan for her.

When your son feels rejected or inadequate, speak words of affirmation to him. Model the love of our heavenly Father in the way you express love to your children.

Never underestimate the power of your influence upon your kids. Love them. Lead them. And equip them to live out the purpose God has prepared for them.

QUESTIONS FOR REFLECTION

1. How are you modeling the love of the heavenly Father in the way you love your child?

2. Is your child finding community in the church? If not, how can you help them do so?

3. How are you helping your child cultivate a sense of purpose?

4. What one thing stood out to you from this article?

MAN AND WOMAN: GOD'S PLAN

The gift of gender is part of the goodness of God's creation.

One of the great parenting challenges of our time is dealing with a generation of children who will grow up in a sexually-confused world. And while the confusion is widespread, one of the primary areas of contention and confusion is the subject of gender. As parents, we must be prepared to help our children move from confusion to clarity by equipping them with a biblical view of sex and gender.

WHAT DOES THE BIBLE SAY?

As we consider the patterns of human sexuality, we must begin by seeking to understand God's purpose and design for humanity. To do this, we look again to the creation story. God created all people to image Him, and He purposefully created us as male and female (Gen. 1:27). Genesis 2 tells us that after God formed Adam from the dust of the earth, for the first time since He began His creative work, He declared something was "not good" (v. 18). God saw that Adam was alone. So He designed a suitable helper for Adam.

From God's creation of Eve, we learn that man and woman were made for each other. As God's image-bearers, they were commanded to "be fruitful, multiply, fill the earth, and subdue it" (Gen. 1:28). Notice that they could only fulfill this command through the complementary bodies they were given. These categories of male and female are neither abstract nor accidental. Our differences are purposeful. In every way, Adam and Eve were designed to be a complementary pair.

For a short time, Adam and Eve enjoyed a perfect relationship with one another, and with God. But very quickly, sin entered the picture. As a result of their sin, Genesis 3 tells us death and a curse were introduced that hindered and disrupted the harmonious, complementary relationship that God had intended for Adam and Eve to enjoy.

But all was not lost at the fall. Jesus came to turn back the curse and its far-reaching effects (Gal. 3:13). And not only that, but in the course of His ministry Jesus reaffirmed the goodness of God's original design for men and women as He taught about marriage in Matthew 19:4-6. Jesus taught that God created us to be male and female and that God's design is still good. And looking even further forward, we learn that it always will be. The Christian vision of salvation pictures men and women standing together in their resurrected bodies in the new heavens and new earth praising God and living together in His eternal kingdom.

Our existence as men and women is not an accident, and it is not a result of sin. God created us to image Him as either male or female, and that pattern is sustained into the new creation.

MASCULINITY AND FEMININITY

Our culture has grown increasingly confused about what defines a man. Rather than challenging or training young men, we are usually content to leave them to idle away adolescence by satisfying sexual urges (through pornography or fornication) and simulating warfare with a game controller. No wonder most young men lack any kind of noble ambition.

The biblical vision of manhood is much more robust and vibrant. God made men to be providers and protectors. Masculinity is an important and God-given feature of manhood. (It is more than OK to encourage our sons to be masculine.) But don't misunderstand. This doesn't have to mean your son is

As parents, we must be prepared to help our children move from confusion to clarity by equipping them with a biblical view of sex and gender.

a deer hunting, truck driving survivalist. The biblical vision of manhood is one of nobility and strength, of sacrifice and courage. A real man fights for what he loves, cherishes the woman God gives him, and pursues the calling God has stamped upon his soul.

According to the Bible, the virtues of manhood are indispensable. In addition to their calling to be strong and faithful (1 Cor. 16:13-14), men are called to exercise spiritual headship in their families (Eph. 5:23). Matt Chandler describes headship as "the unique leadership of the man in the work of establishing order for human flourishing."[3] This is a weighty task. The call to love, serve, protect, and lay down your life for the good of others is the burden of manhood. It cannot be done apart from the Lord's help.

Women have perhaps suffered even more than men at the hands of unhealthy gender stereotypes. They are victims of mixed messaging. If you look around, you will see billboards, commercials, and movies that portray women as barely-clothed sexual objects. At the same time, it is not uncommon to hear protesters and activists declare that women should reject anything distinctly feminine because it supposedly promotes inequality. What a sad message for our daughters.

God's Word paints a much more beautiful picture. Far from denying the value or significance of womanhood, the Bible celebrates it. Proverbs 31 describes "a wife of noble character" (v. 10) as a woman who works hard to provide for her family. She is strong, dignified, and wise (vv. 25-26).

Women bear the image of God in a unique and distinct way. They are not only equal to men, but they represent essential elements of our humanity that would otherwise be absent. They are designed to nurture, serve, and love in a way that creates flourishing in our families and our communities. As parents, we want to teach our daughters (and our sons) about the fullness and beauty of God's plan for women as mothers, wives, daughters, and people.

Men and women are equal and distinct. Both are necessary as they work together to reflect God's image on earth.

GENDER CONFUSION

One of the most important things we can do as parents is to affirm the goodness of God's design to our kids. While the culture sends mixed signals about gender, we must hold fast to the teaching of Scripture.

The culture is confused about gender. In one breath, it praises feminist advances, lifting women up for excelling in a "man's" world. In the next breath, the culture tries to erase gender completely, claiming that male and female are simply labels of self-description, that body parts and chromosomes make no difference.

These incoherent contradictions are a part of a larger pattern that stems from our rebellion and alienation from God. The various aspects of the cultural debate about sexuality and gender are ultimately about what it means to be male and female. In response, we must tirelessly affirm God's design. He made us gendered, embodied, and different. These distinctions are beautiful and they extend to all levels of our being—our emotional, physical and psychological selves—all of it intentional and good.

Christianity doesn't sever gender from sex, because according to the Bible, the unique ways that God made our bodies are tied to our roles. Women are, by nature, more nurturing than men. Men, in contrast, are designed to protect. We should not be ashamed to believe what God, and nature, declares about men and women. His design is beautiful and purposeful, and we should confidently embrace it.

BROKEN IDENTITY

One of the tragic results of the culture's misguided views on sex and gender is the rising number of children and young adults who experience gender dysphoria—when a person feels out of place in their gendered body. The culture tells people that gender is subjective, that is, your gender is determined based on what you believe you are.

If your child should confess that he or she is struggling with this aspect of his or her identity, don't panic. God can redeem this for His glory. As Christian parents, we always want to respond out of love. As you point them to the truth about God's design for men and women, offer grace and compassion.

Here are a few things to keep in mind. First, none of us are the way we are "supposed to be." This is not limited to homosexuality or transgenderism. All people struggle with thoughts and feelings they don't understand and wish they didn't have. Second, surgery is

Be intentional in your home about what it means to be a man or a woman. Talk to your kids about God's design for men and women.

not the solution. One of the consequences of Adam's fall is that we often have desires that do not honor God.

God has given us a blueprint for marriage, sexuality, and relationships. We are not free to deviate from God's plan, no matter how intense our desire or how powerful our logic. God's truth regarding gender dysphoria is simple and straightforward: If you are a man, the desire to become a woman is not from God. These are desires that must be crucified and brought in line with God's will:

Present your bodies as a living sacrifice, holy and pleasing to God; this is your true worship. Do not be conformed to this age, but be transformed by the renewing of your mind, so that you may discern what is the good, pleasing, and perfect will of God.
ROMANS 12:1-2

If our feelings contradict His Word, we must check our feelings, not change our circumstances.

LET YOUR LIFE BE AN EXAMPLE

Be intentional in your home about what it means to be a man or a woman. Talk to your kids about God's design for men and women. Thank God for your son's masculinity or your daughter's femininity when you pray for him or her.

Teach your son to esteem the women and girls in his life and view them as daughters of the King, rather than objects of his desire.

Husbands, build up your wife in front of your kids. Show your sons how you love her and value her. Give your daughter high expectations for how she should be treated by all men. Fathers, teach her what to look for in a godly husband and model this in your home. Don't let her believe her body is only as good as its parts. Her identity and worth are rooted in Christ Jesus.

Remember, the most important things your kids will learn about sex and gender will flow out of the patterns they see at home.

QUESTIONS FOR REFLECTION

1. As a child and teenager, what was modeled and taught to you about what it means to be a man and woman?

2. What is the biblical view of manhood? How is it different than the culture's view? How are you helping your son embrace the biblical view?

3. What is the biblical view of womanhood? How is it different than the culture's view? How are you helping your daughter embrace the biblical view?

4. What one thing stood out to you from this article?

LOSS OF IDENTITY

Mental Health, Depression, and Suicide

MISDIRECTED IDENTITY

Life is hard and full of disappointment. From not making the team, to losing a treasured possession, to being passed over for a part in the play, or just failing to fit in, our children are guaranteed to experience heartache and disappointment as they grow up. Life doesn't always meet our expectations.

Loneliness is a major difficulty in the lives of young people. Our kids want to be known and to have an identity in this world. The desire to fit in exhibits enormous pressure from their earliest years. The need to belong can override logic, knowledge, belief, and even their sense of self. And the unfortunate result of looking to others for validation and approval is that you inevitably lose sight of your identity in Christ.

Deeper issues like anxiety, depression, and thoughts of suicide are also related to the problem of misdirected identity. As Christ-centered parents, we must be aware of these dangers and be prepared to point our kids back to Christ.

WHAT DOES THE BIBLE SAY?

God created us to be truly and fully human (John 10:10). The breadth and depth of the emotions we experience are one of the most important aspects of our humanity. Our emotions are not a result of sin or the fall. The emotions we feel—such as wonder, anger, happiness, peace, and sorrow—are not only essential to our lives, they are also seen in the life and ministry of Jesus (Matt. 8:10; John 11:33-35; Heb. 5:7).

Unfortunately, because of the fall our emotions are sometimes misdirected by sin. This shows up in various ways, but often sin attempts to direct our affections toward idols (Col. 3:5). Our kids may struggle with feelings of loneliness or depression. Sin will drive them to seek relief from these feelings through false gods like sex, drugs, or the approval of others, instead of seeking comfort and validation in Jesus.

The fall has brought sin and brokenness, even to our emotions. The hope of the gospel is that the people of God are awaiting a future kingdom where there will be no more "grief, crying, and pain" (Rev. 21:4). So we wait for the day when we will be like Jesus, fully human in every way, but free from sin and hurt and pain.

WHAT IS NORMAL?

As we think through issues related to identity and mental health, it is important to develop a realistic picture of what *normal* is. "The 'normal' human life isn't what is marketed to us by the pharmaceutical industry or by the lives we see projected on movie screens, or, frankly, by a lot of Christian sermons and praise songs."[4] Sadly, many of our churches have taught children to mask emotion rather than express it in a healthy manner by projecting superficial happiness in our sermons and worship songs and diminishing the role of lament.

Far from triumphalism—placing too much emphasis on the joys of life while diminishing the effects of sin—"*the normal human life is the life of Jesus of Nazareth,* who sums up in himself everything it means to be human (Eph. 1:10). And the life of Christ presented to us in the Gospels is a life of joy, fellowship and celebration, but also of loneliness, profound sadness, lament, grief, anger and suffering, all without sin."[5]

Perfectionism robs our kids of joy. The gospel message should free our kids from the prison of perfectionism. In His earthly ministry, Jesus welcomed sinners to the dinner table (Mark 2:15). He didn't check their sin registry or happiness levels at the door. He knew their failures and He invited them in to experience Him.

When your kid is hurting, the aim is not to fix him or return him to some illusive state of normal. Point him to Jesus:

Let us run with endurance the race that lies before us, keeping our eyes on Jesus, the source and perfecter of our faith. For the joy that lay before him, he endured the cross, despising the shame, and sat down at the right hand of the throne of God.

HEBREWS·12:1a-2

Turning to Christ to find our value and self-worth requires us to reject the temptation to pursue significance by chasing after idols. We should count it all joy as we destroy those idols and grow into completeness in Christ (Jas. 1:2-4).

MENTAL HEALTH

Thinking about our own children suffering with mental health issues is scary. There are two common mistakes parents make. One mistake is to assume these issues will never affect our children. The second mistake is to assume that there is nothing you can do if they should suffer in this way. Don't be afraid. The hope of the gospel is stronger than your fear.

These are real issues. More than six million teens in the U.S. have been diagnosed with an anxiety disorder, which is twenty-five percent of the teen population. In 2015, 12.5 percent of adolescents ages twelve to seventeen had at least one major depressive episode. That number was up from 4.6 percent in 2006.[6]

While Christians have a wide range of views on addressing mental health issues, we all agree that prayer is essential. This does not exclude taking advantage of modern medicine when appropriate. If depression and anxiety are brought on by physiological reasons, medicine may help to alleviate negative symptoms. But in every case, we pray for God to comfort our spirits and remind ourselves that Jesus is our peace:

The peace of God, which surpasses all understanding, will guard your hearts and minds in Christ Jesus.
PHILIPPIANS 4:7

It is especially important for Christian parents to be mindful that the purpose of many anti-depressants is merely to suppress symptoms—not to rid the body of the source of depression.

Your child may be walking through a period of grief or guilt caused by sin. In this case, medicine will not resolve the issue. Be in tune to your child's circumstances. Determine the cause of depression before determining treatment.

WARNING SIGNS

How do you know when your child is suffering from anxiety or depression? Emotions and social behavior can help clue you in to your child's state of mind. Watch for these warning signs:

• Extreme sadness or withdrawal from friends and activities

• Having intense worries or fears that affect daily activities

• Out-of-character aggressive behavior—getting into fights, hurting others, or hurting self

• Not eating or throwing up after eating; rapid weight loss

• Substance abuse

Anxiety and depression often come as a result of life situations that are difficult for children to process. This might include the death of a loved one, divorce or separation of parents, or major transitions (new home or school). Also be on guard if your child is experiencing teasing or bullying at school or is having problems fitting in.[7]

Even young children are not immune to loneliness and anxiety. Pay attention to symptoms to determine if your child's sadness is a passing mood or something more severe that might require your involvement.

SUICIDE

Approximately forty-four thousand people die by suicide each year and almost five hundred thousand people are estimated to attempt suicide each year.[8] As of 2015, suicide was the second leading cause of death for people ages ten to twenty-four.[9]

Suicide is tragic. It disregards the image of God and the sanctity of human life. It denies God's sovereignty over one's body and leaves behind a trail of loss, grief, and guilt. And it

While you tell your children they are loved and intimately known by the Creator God, believe it for yourself.

almost always occurs in response to suffering or the anticipation of suffering. Suicide is an attempt to escape the pain that comes from living in a broken world. Purposely ending one's life through suicide fails to recognize the hope and comfort that is offered to us in Jesus.

How do you help your child when they confess thoughts of suicide? First, pray for God's mercy and help. Thank them for reaching out. Asking for help is an act of courage. Try to ask questions in order to understand the situation. Gently and lovingly attempt to discern the severity and duration of these thoughts. And seek to determine if they have the means to commit suicide or have attempted suicide in the past.

Remind them of the presence of Christ that gives us hope in our darkest moments. Finally, connect them to help. Find a trusted pastor or biblical counselor who can give loving care that will lead to restored health.

TAKE ACTION

Ultimately, we want the feelings of loneliness, worthlessness, and despair to be replaced with hope in Jesus Christ, "a sure and steadfast anchor of the soul" (Heb. 6:19). We want to help our kids to overcome the effects of sin and feel whole and complete in Christ.

As parents we should pray, study God's Word, seek godly counsel, and lean on the power of the Holy Spirit. You are not in this parenting journey alone. While you tell your children that they are loved and intimately known by the Creator God, believe it for yourself. God is with you, guiding you to raise up the kids He gave you.

Don't shy away from difficult topics like identity and mental health with your kids. These conversations must happen. You want the answers they are seeking to come from you, not social media, television, or even their peers. They need the hope of the gospel. They need to know the story of the One who gave His life "so that they may have life and have it in abundance" (John 10:10).

Pray for your children and prepare yourself to walk with them through all the challenges of life.

QUESTIONS FOR REFLECTION

1. How have you seen your child deal with disappointment?

2. Are you pushing your child toward perfectionism or helping him or her be free from it?

3. What are you currently doing to prepare yourself to help your child deal with any mental health issues?

4. What is one thing that stood out to you from this article?

BIG IDEA

As your child learns about the world around him, ground your preschooler's identity in who God created him or her to be.

KEY SCRIPTURES

- *You are fearfully and wonderfully made* (Ps. 139:13-14).
- *You are made in God's image* (Gen. 1:27).
- *God created us as girls and boys/men and women* (Gen. 1:27).
- *You are a child of God* (1 John 3:1).

KEY QUESTIONS YOUR PRESCHOOLER IS ASKING

- Who am I?
- What is this big world around me?
- Why are people different?

AT THIS AGE MOST PRESCHOOLERS WILL ...

- Label themselves as a boy or a girl.
- Have a stable sense of their gender identity.
- Learn gender role behavior, i.e. doing "things that boys do" or identifying certain toys as "for girls."

DEVELOPMENTAL MILESTONES

- A preschooler is *curious*. He learns by using all of his senses to explore the world around him.
- A preschooler is *sensitive*. Though she cannot verbalize her feelings, a preschooler can read the emotions and feelings around her. She needs a consistent, positive environment to help her grow.
- A preschooler is *literal-minded*. He thinks in terms of what he has seen and experienced. He understands words only in their concrete meanings. The use of symbolic or figurative language at home or church may confuse him.
- A preschooler *explores limits* for two reasons. First, she wants greater independence. Second, she wants to be reassured that her environment is safe. Frequently, preschoolers who push the limits do so because the limits are always moving and changing. When parents and teachers have different expectations for

behavior, the child is confused and will automatically begin to search for new boundaries. As the child questions limits in her experiences, provide firm but loving guidance to ensure safety and a secure environment.

COACHING TIPS

- Listen to your preschooler's feelings. Help him identify his emotions. Discuss the causes of and solutions to bad feelings.
- Remind your child of God's truths often. Encourage ways for her to remember the difference between her feelings and God's truth.
- Emphasize that differences do not make a person better or worse. Discuss differences she notices in others. Explain that God made everyone unique.
- Continually affirm that God designed him to be who he is.

CONVERSATION STARTERS

- **GOD MADE YOU SPECIAL.** What are some things you love to do? Let your child know God created her with special talents and gifts. Provide opportunities for her to explore those talents and gifts.
- **WE GO TO CHURCH TOGETHER.** What do you like to do at church? Use any family moment to emphasize the importance of family identity rooted in Christ.
- **WHAT ARE YOUR FAVORITE THINGS TO DO TOGETHER?** Family activities, whether on a drive or at the dinner table, are perfect opportunities to model and discuss the role of different values you observe in your family.

SAY OR PRAY

- God created you and said everything He made is good.
- God created you for a special job.
- God created you as a boy or a girl.
- God created many different kinds of people.

BIG IDEA

Ground your child's identity in Christ rather than what the media says, friends say, or based on what he or she does or doesn't do.

KEY SCRIPTURES

- *You are fearfully and wonderfully made* (Ps. 139:13-14).
- *You are made in God's image* (Gen. 1:27).
- *God created us as girls and boys/men and women* (Gen. 1:27).
- *You are a child of God* (1 John 3:1).
- *You have a purpose* (Matt. 22:37-39).

KEY QUESTIONS YOUR ELEMENTARY-AGED CHILD IS ASKING

- Who am I?
- What does it mean to be _____ (race, religion, gender)?
- Why are people different?

AT THIS AGE MOST ELEMENTARY CHILDREN WILL ...

- Act out traits associated with their gender through appearance, social behavior, physical behavior, and social relationships.
- Begin to prefer playtime and activities they associate with members of their own gender.

DEVELOPMENTAL MILESTONES

- At this age, your child will begin to absorb messages from media, culture, and friends that shape his identity, so it's incredibly important to reinforce his unique worth, both to you as parents and to God. Model and discuss a moral lifestyle often, and compare what the media says to what the Bible says is true.
- Routines are important to your child, providing a sense of security, happiness, and self-confidence. These attributes can also be attained through healthy activities, like sports, arts, or academics.
- God gave your child a unique purpose, so use every opportunity to capitalize on her individual strengths and characteristics—both verbally and in the activities you encourage.
- Be mindful of your child's unique needs, such as ADHD or perfectionism, and point out healthy ways to manage his impulses or behavior.

- Be careful not to try to change your child's personality to fit a social norm; instead, find a balance between nurturing her natural inclinations and promoting new shaping behaviors.
- Most importantly, always keep the focus on God. Praying out loud for your child where he can hear will set a good example of submitting to God as well as building his self-concept as he learns that God cares for him.

COACHING TIPS

- Always listen to your child's feelings. Help her identify those feelings. Discuss the causes of and solutions to bad feelings.
- Remind your child of God's truths often. Encourage ways for him to remember the difference between his feelings and God's truth.
- Emphasize that differences do not make a person better or worse. Discuss differences she notices in others. Explain that God made everyone unique.
- Maintain an open environment so your child will always feel comfortable to talk to you about himself.

CONVERSATION STARTERS

- **YOU ARE TALENTED AT THIS! WHY DO YOU THINK GOD GAVE YOU THIS TALENT?** Anytime your child accomplishes something, talk about her strengths and the virtues she used to achieve her goal. Bring up how God made her with special talents, and ask her about ways she could use those talents to honor Him.
- **WHAT IS YOUR FAVORITE THING WE DO EVERY WEEK TOGETHER AS A FAMILY?** Use any family moment to emphasize the importance of family identity rooted in Christ. Family activities, whether on a drive or at the dinner table, are perfect opportunities to model and discuss the role of different values you observe in your family.
- **TELL ME ONE GOOD THING AND ONE BAD THING THAT HAPPENED TODAY.** Rather than asking how your child's day was, engage in discussion by asking about his "highs and lows" of the day—the best part and the worst part. The high point is an opportunity to talk about having a grateful heart, and the low point could be a chance to explore ways to honor God even when bad things happen or when your child is unhappy.

SAY OR PRAY

- God created you and said everything He made is good.
- God created you as a boy or a girl.
- God created all different kinds of people and each with a special job.
- God loves everyone and sent Jesus to die for all people all over the world.

BIG IDEA

Ground your preteen's identity in Christ rather than what the world says, his or her feelings, or what peers say to your preteen.

KEY SCRIPTURES

- *You are fearfully and wonderfully made in God's image* (Gen. 1:27; Ps. 139:13-14).
- *You are a child of God* (1 John 3:1).
- *You have a purpose* (Matt. 22:37-39).
- *Your body is a temple of the Holy Spirit* (1 Cor. 6:19-20).

KEY QUESTIONS YOUR PRETEEN MAY ASK

- Who am I?
- What is my purpose?
- Why do I feel this way?

AT THIS AGE MOST PRETEENS WILL …

- Be generally comfortable with who they are but are more aware of what others think.
- See friends as a source of support and happiness.
- Try to figure out what is right and wrong.

DEVELOPMENTAL MILESTONES

- Your preteen is beginning to be influenced more by others around him. Do your best to surround your child with a nourishing social environment and healthy relationships. While monitoring friendships, try not to judge any social interactions too quickly. This could damage communication with your child.
- Preteens may focus on body image and things they do not like about themselves. Hurtful comments and bullying of any kind can deepen this crisis. As a parent, giving constant positive feedback is crucial to reinforce your preteen's identity in Christ as a special creation who God loves and sent His Son, Jesus, to save.
- Model and discuss a righteous lifestyle often and examine any lies or deception the media dictates about sin. Take every opportunity to focus on healthy values, like integrity, hard work, responsibility, and kindness.
- A sense of belonging is extremely important in this stage, so respecting her budding sense of independence is also crucial. Be sure to constantly emphasize God's love for and acceptance of her.

- God gave your child a unique purpose, so praise good decisions your child makes, emphasizing how important good character is.
- Be mindful of your child's unique needs or emotions, as depression, anxiety, and loneliness are common during this stage of development. Be sensitive to mood swings, but also stay vigilant for signs of more serious behavior. Affirm that you will always love your child regardless of the situation.
- Most importantly, always keep the focus on God. Praying together can keep an open channel of spiritual communication. It is important for preteens to understand their identity and purpose are in Christ, so discuss this often.

COACHING TIPS

- Listen closely to your preteen's feelings. Discuss causes and solutions of bad feelings, highlighting prayer and time with God as an important resolution.
- Remind your child of God's truths often. Encourage ways for her to remember the difference between her feelings and God's truth.
- Be vulnerable with your preteen. If he knows you truly understand his emotions, he will trust you more; so don't be afraid to be real with him.
- Maintain your composure to keep dialogue open. Your preteen may try to shock you or hide things from you, fearful of telling you.

CONVERSATION STARTERS

- **TELL ME ABOUT YOUR FAVORITE TV SHOW, MOVIE, OR MUSIC.** Engage in conversations that pertain to your child's interests. Emotionally connecting with a preteen can sometimes be challenging, so discuss a topic she is passionate about and find focal points where you can segue into deeper conversation.
- **LET'S GO DO THIS TOGETHER.** Find an activity to do together with your child. When your child can relax and have fun with you, he is more likely to be honest or come to you with questions.
- **WHAT WAS THE HIGH POINT AND LOW POINT OF YOUR DAY?** Rather than asking how your child's day was, begin discussion by asking about the best part and the worst part. Ask nonjudgmental, open-ended questions about your child's answers. Try to avoid questions that begin with "Why," as they often put kids on the defensive.

SAY OR PRAY

- God created you in His image to reflect Him.
- God created you for a specific purpose.
- God created you as a boy or a girl for a reason.
- God created you to show His love to others.

BIG IDEA

Your middle schooler's identity is to be rooted in and defined by who he or she is in Jesus.

KEY SCRIPTURES

- *When we receive Christ, we become children of God* (John 1:12).
- *As children of God, we are becoming more like Christ* (Rom. 12:1-2; 2 Cor. 3:18).
- *Our acceptance of others isn't based on their actions. It's based on Christ's acceptance of us* (Rom. 15:7).

KEY QUESTIONS YOUR MIDDLE SCHOOLER IS ASKING

- Who am I?
- Why do I feel left out and like I don't fit in?
- Why am I so lonely and sad all the time?
- How do I interact with students who are struggling with sexual identity?

AT THIS AGE MOST MIDDLE SCHOOLERS WILL …

- Feel pressure to acquire peer approval and affirmation.
- Struggle with issues of personal identity, especially in light of what they have done and what has been done to them.
- Begin to engage more on a personal level with the social controversies in our culture, such as issues related to gender, mental health, and so forth.

DEVELOPMENTAL MILESTONES

- Middle schoolers learn best when they see the practical side and how it impacts them directly. Make a point to talk about how a proper understanding of their identity in Christ impacts every part of their life.
- Middle schoolers are physically growing at different rates. These are awkward years. He may be embarrassed easily and need to talk about his feelings, even when his face says otherwise.
- Middle schoolers are beginning to have capability to wrestle with deeper things of the faith. They are able to comprehend doctrines, beliefs, the full narrative of Scripture, and how these things apply to their lives.

PARENTS OF MIDDLE SCHOOLERS

COACHING TIPS

- Know that the middle school years can be a difficult time of life. It's very possible your middle schooler will come to you with serious questions like: *What is wrong with me? Why am I so lonely? Why don't other kids like me? What type of person will I turn out to be?* Be a good listener, be patient, and be willing to walk with her through this awkward time. Even if she struggles to ask these questions, work to create an environment where she feels freedom to ask them. Pour out much love and encouragement, continually assuring her of her worth and value to you and to God.
- In this time of your middle schooler's faith formation, share the ups and downs of your own faith story. Talk to him about what it means to find his identity in Christ.
- Your middle schooler is not ignorant of how the current culture is defining manhood and womanhood. Hopefully you've already started the discussion about what the Bible says about being a man and a woman, but if not, it's time to start now. And remember, your middle schooler is going to learn about biblical manhood and womanhood not only from what she hears, but also from what she sees.

CONVERSATION STARTERS

- **WHEN DO YOU FEEL MOST PRESSURED BY YOUR FRIENDS TO THINK OR ACT A CERTAIN WAY?** This question will help you assess how much influence your middle schooler's peer group has on him. Since his peer group is becoming increasingly important to him, do your best to know who his friends are.
- **WHO IS THE BEST MAN/WOMAN YOU KNOW?** Find out who your middle schooler looks to as the best model for manhood and womanhood. Ask her why she chose that particular person and note what characteristics your middle schooler sees as valuable. Use the conversation to uphold and discuss biblical manhood and womanhood.
- **WHAT DO YOU REALLY LOVE TO DO?** Discuss what your middle schooler is becoming passionate about and how you can support him in this activity.

SAY OR PRAY

- Pray that your middle schooler finds her identity in Christ and not in how she performs or what others say about her.
- Pray God would surround your middle schooler with godly influences, including friends and other significant adults to speak into his life.
- Ask the Lord to give you wisdom and patience as you guide your middle schooler through this time in her life.

BIG IDEA

Your high schooler's identity is to be rooted in and defined by who he or she is in Jesus.

KEY SCRIPTURES

- *When we receive Christ, we become children of God* (John 1:12).
- *As children of God, we are becoming more like Christ* (Rom. 8:29; 12:1-2; 2 Cor. 3:18).
- *Our acceptance of others isn't based on their actions. It's based on Christ's acceptance of us* (Rom. 15:7).

KEY QUESTIONS YOUR HIGH SCHOOLER IS ASKING

- Who am I?
- Where do I fit in?
- Why is there so much pressure to perform?
- Is it wrong for people to change genders?

AT THIS AGE MOST HIGH SCHOOLERS WILL …

- Have numerous influences shaping their identities, including parents, family, church, peers, and culture.
- Feel more pressure to live up to expectations set by themselves, parents, coaches, friends, and so forth.
- Still often feel strange about who they are and their bodies.

DEVELOPMENTAL MILESTONES

- High schoolers experience a changing relationship with parents as they try to balance independence with connection. They struggle with the desire to separate, while not wanting to let go of their parents' comfort and protection.
- At this age, your high schoolers' relationships with friends competes with the relationship with you. The peer relationships will exert a greater influence than parents in many situations, including identity formation. This is especially the case in romantic relationships.
- A high schooler is becoming better equipped to make important decisions. However, continued brain development and lack of maturity can lead to making rash decisions without considering the consequences.

COACHING TIPS

- Recognize the changing relationship with your teenager as he stretches toward leaving your home. Find ways to provide him more independence in his decision-making and responsibilities without totally cutting him loose.
- Your high schooler is being bombarded with the wrong definitions the culture is voicing about what it means to be a man and what it means to be a woman. Model and teach biblical manhood and womanhood. Discuss this in dedicated times of instruction and in spontaneous teachable moments.
- While encouraging your high schooler to excel in academics, sports, music, and other activities, caution her about getting so consumed with these things that she finds her identity in them.
- Do all you can to teach and reinforce that your high schooler's identity is based on who she is in Christ. To do this, you're going to need to understand what that means for yourself.
- It's OK to encourage and challenge your high schooler to reach high. However, be careful not to demand he reach unattainable goals. You don't want to give the impression that your love or your high schooler's worth is based on his performance. Also, make sure you're not vicariously living life through your high schooler.

CONVERSATION STARTERS

- **TO YOU, WHAT DOES IT MEAN TO BE A MAN? TO BE A WOMAN?** Listen closely to gauge whether the culture's voice or the biblical voice is louder in your high schooler's life. Work to make this an ongoing conversation.
- **WHAT ARE SOME THINGS YOU REALLY LIKE ABOUT YOURSELF? IF YOU COULD CHANGE ONE THING ABOUT YOURSELF, WHAT WOULD IT BE?** These questions will help you evaluate how your high schooler feels about herself. Continue to remind her that her worth and value are found in Christ.
- **WHAT LABELS ARE PLACED ON PEOPLE AT SCHOOL?** You can steer this discussion to find out if your high schooler is being labeled and how those labels are affecting him.

SAY OR PRAY

- Pray that your high schooler will find her true identity in Christ.
- Acknowledging the amount of influence friends have on your high schooler, pray that he would surround himself with godly friends who will encourage him toward Jesus.
- Repent of placing undue pressure on your high schooler and basing your love and affection on her performance. See her and love her as Christ does.

BIG IDEA

Your young adult's identity is to be rooted in and defined by who he or she is in Jesus.

KEY SCRIPTURES

- *When we receive Christ, we become children of God* (John 1:12).
- *As children of God, we are becoming more like Christ* (Rom. 8:29; 12:1-2; 2 Cor. 3:18).
- *Our acceptance of others isn't based on their actions. It's based on Christ's acceptance of us* (Rom. 15:7).

KEY QUESTIONS YOUR YOUNG ADULT IS ASKING

- Who am I?
- What is my purpose in life?
- How do I find acceptance?
- Why do I feel as if my identity is wrapped up in my accomplishments? How can I avoid becoming a failure?

AT THIS AGE MOST YOUNG ADULTS WILL …

- More personally encounter social controversies in our culture, such as issues related to gender, mental health, and so forth.
- Be wrestling with questions about their purpose in life.
- Feel more pressure to acquire peer approval and affirmation.
- Still be struggling with issues of personal identity, especially in light of what they have done and what has been done to them.

DEVELOPMENTAL MILESTONES

- Young adults will move from identifying themselves as extensions of their parents to realizing they are unique individuals.
- Although young adults will have a firmer sense of identity, they will still be exploring identity in different areas, such as personal relationships, education, vocation, and so forth.
- They will go through a time of feeling "in-between"—no longer a kid but not quite an adult. Unfortunately, sometimes the place they experience this the most is at church.

COACHING TIPS

• Create an environment where your young adult can ask tough questions like: *What's wrong with me? Why am I so depressed? What type of person will I turn out to be? Why can't I get this habit under control?* Make sure you give prayerful, measured, and biblical answers to help them navigate these issues.

• Be aware that your young adult may always want to put his best foot forward. He may always paint a pretty picture, even if things in his life are going south. So don't take everything he tells you at face value. You may need to dig deeper by observing actions, decisions, and habits.

• Encourage your young adult to excel, but be careful not to give off the message that your love for her is tied up in her accomplishment or performance.

• Continue to help your young adult find his identity in Christ. Discuss together what that means. Make sure you have a good grasp of the concept and are applying it in your own life before talking with your young adult about it.

CONVERSATION STARTERS

• **BASED ON WHAT YOU HEAR AND SEE IN MEDIA, HOW DOES OUR CULTURE DEFINE WHAT IT MEANS TO BE A MAN OR A WOMAN?** This question should open the door to talk about biblical manhood and womanhood. Be careful not to revert to gender stereotypes.

• **DO YOU FEEL LIKE I'VE PUSHED YOU TOO HARD IN SOME AREAS?** This may be a difficult question to ask, and even more difficult to hear the answer. But hopefully the hard truth will begin healing wounds that you may not have even realized you inflicted.

• **DO YOU EVER FEEL TEMPTED TO BASE YOUR IDENTITY ON THE THINGS YOU HAVE DONE OR THE THINGS THAT HAVE BEEN DONE TO YOU?** Hopefully this discussion moves to talk about what it means to find our identity in Christ.

SAY OR PRAY

• Pray your young adult will find his identity in Christ.

• Pray for yourself to have strength to model and live biblical manhood or womanhood. Pray your young adult would do the same.

SESSION 4
SEXUALITY

PROVIDING A GODLY PERSPECTIVE ON SEX

Use the space below to record notes, quotes, thoughts, and questions from the video panel discussion.

_____

_____

_____

_____

_____

_____

_____

_____

_____

_____

_____

_____

_____

_____

_____

_____

_____

_____

_____

_____

_____

_____

_____

_____

_____

_____

_____

GROUP GUIDE

Use the following questions and prompts to continue the conversation about the issues discussed by the video panel.

How was the topic of sex dealt with in your home growing up? Is that different than how it's being dealt with in your home today? Explain.

What did Ben Stuart mean when he talked about championing the positive when talking about sex with your children, especially with teens and young adults? Why is this important?

Do you have a "no shame" culture in your home where every question is OK to ask? Explain. How do you build that kind of culture?

When are the best times for you to have serious conversations with your child? How do you take advantage of these?

Why is it important that you talk specifically about sex with your child, not abstractly? Is this difficult for you? Why or why not?

Jackie Hill Perry said that when we talk about purity with our children, we should talk more about God than about sex. What did she mean? Do you agree? Explain.

Are you currently talking about same-sex attraction with your child? Why or why not? If so, how are you approaching it?

How can we value people who identify as gay, lesbian, or transgender, without embracing or endorsing their lifestyle? Is your home a safe place to discuss this? Explain.

What are some actions you can take to combat pornography in your home? Which of these actions are you currently doing?

If your teen revealed to you, or it came to your attention that he or she was sexually active, how would you respond?

How can you foster a continuing conversation about sexuality in your home?

TAKEAWAYS:

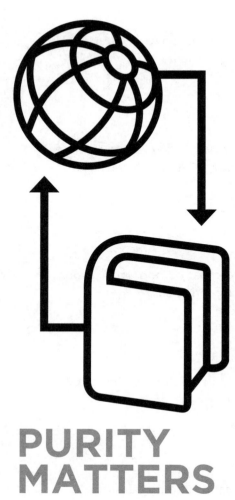

PURITY MATTERS

"Our bodies have been created not just by God. Our bodies have been created for God." This culture "screams at every turn, 'Please your body.' The Bible shouts at every turn, 'Please God.'"[1]

If what the world offers is so appealing, why does purity matter? The fact is, the modern sexual revolution is making promises it can't keep. Satan's great lie has always been, "You can have all this—everything you desire—and you will not surely die," but this is a lie that leads to destruction (Prov. 14:12).

As parents, we want to be the ones who shape and influence the way that our children think about sex. The culture will constantly tell our kids that sex is everything. We need to be prepared to guide them toward the truth—not in a single conversation, but with ongoing conversations—about sex and sexuality and how God intends for both to fit into our lives.

WHAT DOES THE BIBLE SAY?

Humans are embodied beings. We were created by God and we bear His image in the world. He also created both sex and sexuality. Sometimes we are tempted to think that these things are inherently bad, but that isn't true. Even before the fall of man, we see a picture of Adam and Eve joined together as one flesh. From that scene in the garden, we see both sexes (Adam and Eve as male and female) and their sexuality (Adam and Eve united in sexual union) were all without sin. In fact, the author of Genesis comments positively, "Both the man and his wife were naked, yet felt no shame" (Gen. 2:25).

But because of the fall, sin affects every aspect of our existence—even our sexual desires. And because our sexual desires are often misdirected, we live in a world full of sexual sin. The culture lives by the premise that we can do "whatever, whenever" with the bodies the Lord gave us and that denying our desires is harmful and repressive. But Scripture plainly tells us "the body is not for sexual immorality but

As Christians, we want to take a redemptive view of sex. Through the gospel, God not only redeems our brokenness, but He also enables us to experience the intended goodness of our sexuality.

for the Lord" (1 Cor. 6:13). Because of sin, we often have desires that simply should not be obeyed (Rom. 7). We know that our desires are fleeting, so we need something better than desire to determine how we use our bodies. We need the Word of God.

The Bible's teachings on sexual immorality are crystal clear:

Flee sexual immorality! Every other sin a person commits is outside the body, but the person who is sexually immoral sins against his own body. Don't you know that your body is a temple of the Holy Spirit who is in you, whom you have from God? You are not your own, for you were bought at a price. So glorify God with your body.
1 CORINTHIANS 6:18-20

We will not live by a biblical sexual ethic unless we believe that our bodies are temples of the Holy Spirit because of the redemptive work of Christ.

As Christians, we want to take a redemptive view of sex. Through the gospel, God not only redeems our brokenness, but He also enables us to experience the intended goodness of our sexuality. We have to guard against two opposite errors: We must not be pulled in by the culture's distorted view of sex, but we must also refuse to talk about sex as if it's anything less than a God-given gift.

The apostle Paul said in Colossians,

Therefore, put to death what belongs to your earthly nature: sexual immorality, impurity, lust, evil desire, and greed, which is idolatry. Because of these, God's wrath is coming upon the disobedient.
COLOSSIANS 3:5-6

Flee. Put to death. Paul was adamant that we must get as far away from these sins as possible because they are utterly destructive. Sexual immorality isn't only physically and emotionally damaging; it is a desecration of God's holy dwelling place—our body.

At the same time, the Bible nowhere indicates that sex or sexuality are in any way negative. We want our children to know that sex is a gift from God (that is harmful apart from His design). We want them to desire to experience the pleasures of sex as God intended, within the covenant of marriage. And we want to teach them to honor God with their bodies. How might a biblically faithful vision of sex help your children determine what they will do with their bodies?

This will obviously require additional conversation if one of your children does not know the Lord. This doesn't mean we avoid talking about sexual morality with a child who has not yet placed their faith in Christ, but we cannot expect him or her to fully embrace a Christian sexual ethic without the direction of the Holy Spirit. If

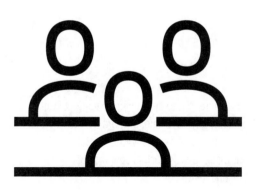

your child is not a Christian, pray for your child's salvation and keep the gospel central in your conversations.

MORE THAN ABSTINENCE

When we talk about purity, our conversation usually defaults to what you should not do. Kids want to know, "How far is too far?" Asking this question is missing the point. It's flirting with sin, seeing how close we can get to the line without putting a toe over it. Paul said, "Flee." This is about honoring God with our bodies, not getting by on a technicality.

What we mean is that purity actually matters. A message that merely begs our kids to hang in there until the wedding day is horribly inadequate. In between your son or daughter's first inkling of sexual temptation and the enjoyment of holy, married sex, sin will constantly seek to create temptations that can severely damage the heart and soul of your child. The goal for our children is not just avoiding sexual activity; the goal is holiness.

We need to help our kids think through how sexual purity relates to other parts of their spiritual life. We also need to prepare

them for the severity of the sexual temptations they are likely to face. These are difficult challenges. Our sexual desires are good. They are given to us by God. But sin preys on these desires and uses them to draw us into sexual immorality. Parents, you can do so much to help your child fight against sexual temptation simply by being there for them and being willing to talk to them about these issues. Reject the temptation to be evasive with your child when talking about sexual temptation.

When kids fall into sexual sin, it produces shame which often leads to more sin. Open the conversation. Help them think about what they should—and should not—be doing in regard to sexual purity, while helping them pursue holiness in all areas of life.

SETTING BOUNDARIES

Sexual sin is going to be a temptation for your child at some point. Experiencing this temptation is normal:

No temptation has come upon you except what is common to humanity. But God is faithful; he will not allow you to be tempted beyond what you are able, but with the temptation he will also provide a way out so that you may be able to bear it.
1 CORINTHIANS 10:13

But how do they handle temptation when it comes? Are they putting themselves in compromising situations? What boundaries should you put in place for your kids? Dean Inserra writes:

There is one purpose and one purpose only for what is known as "foreplay." … The purpose is that it prepares you for and leads you to sex. It was not designed to stop before a climax. It is absolutely what the Scriptures would designate as "sexual immorality." … We've got to get serious about sexual sin. Sex, foreplay, nakedness, etc., are not for dating people, in love people, or mature people, but for married people. … God is not trying to keep you from something; He's saving you from something. Let's believe that He does truly know best.[2]

Adolescents need guidance. Physically, they may feel as if they are ready for sex, but cognitively they are not able to process all the possible consequences of their actions. Our rational ability to make moral decisions are not fully developed until early adulthood. Setting boundaries helps protect our kids from situations they are not emotionally or mentally ready for. As parents, it is our job to take the lead with our kids in setting these boundaries and determining what is appropriate.

LOVE AND GRACE

Educate your children in age-appropriate ways about sexuality. Begin early by giving young children a clear framework that our bodies belong to the Lord (1 Cor. 6:19). (Note: This is important in setting the stage to talk about sexual abuse later on.)

When you approach this subject in conversation, don't feel like you have to make it an event. Talking with your kids about sex is awkward enough already. Make sure your kids know you are available to answer questions when they have them. They will have questions. You want to be the one they go to first.

Let your son or daughter know you've walked in their shoes. You don't have to go into too many details. But let them know you understand and that they won't be shamed for struggling with sin. Your kids will mess up. Be ready to offer abundant supplies of grace.

Establish an atmosphere of love in your home so your kids don't ever feel like they need to search for it somewhere else. The world will tell them that sex is love. Show them Christ is the Source of true satisfaction. Help your kids feel love and acceptance through both your words and your actions.

At the end of the day, we must not only hand down a list of rules—we must help our children understand why purity matters. Purity matters because we belong to the Lord.

QUESTIONS FOR REFLECTION

1. Up to this point, how effective have you been at helping your child understand and live by a biblical view of sex?

2. How is purity more than just abstinence?

3. What kind of boundaries for sexual purity have you set for your child and how are you doing at helping them stay within those boundaries?

4. What one thing stood out to you from this article?

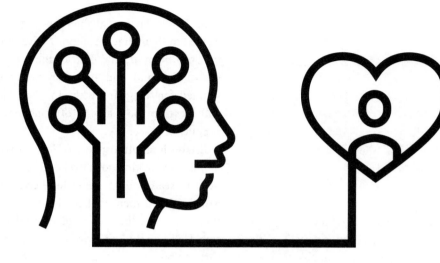

SAME-SEX ATTRACTION AND HOMOSEXUALITY

Whatever defined us before coming to Christ no longer defines us in Christ. And one day, by His grace, we will be made whole.[3]

HOMOSEXUALITY

Sexual sin is not a new problem, neither is the issue of homosexuality. But it's easy to see that times have changed. Homosexuality is now championed by the media, cemented into law, and public opinion—especially among younger generations—has turned decidedly in support of it. According to the culture, anyone who continues to defend traditional sexual ethics is on "the wrong side of history."

There is some good news. Humans have always transgressed the limits of God's design for marriage and sexuality. Despite these challenges, marriage has proved resilient throughout human history. The reason

is simple: Marriage was designed by God to picture the gospel. Biblical sexual ethics may be regarded as both outdated and unloving, but Christians should not be concerned about the way history will regard our fidelity to God's plan for human sexuality. The arc of history is long, and it points in one direction—toward the fulfillment of God's redemptive work in Christ.

As parents, we can confidently tell our children about God's intentions for love and sexuality. We do not need to adjust our views to adhere to the wisdom of the culture, nor do we need to shelter our kids from these cultural realities. Instead, we can help our kids navigate the challenges related to sexual brokenness by pointing them to the beauty of God's design.

WHAT DOES THE BIBLE SAY?

When we think about the Bible's teaching on human sexuality, we follow the lead of Jesus who affirms the creational design of marriage in Matthew 19:1-10. In that passage, Jesus pointed out that marriage—the union of one man to one woman—was instituted by God and intended to last a lifetime. Marriage itself points to the gospel. God established the institution of marriage to picture the relationship of "Christ and the church" (Eph. 5:32). God also established marriage so that human beings could experience love and sexual intimacy in ways that are appropriate and honoring to Him (1 Cor. 7:1-9).

Too often we are tempted to wade into conversations about homosexuality or same-sex attraction apart from consideration of the broader biblical teaching on sexuality. Having seen that both sexuality and marriage were designed by God as a part of His plan for humanity, it is then possible to engage the topics of homosexuality and same-sex attraction as issues that deviate from God's overall pattern for sex and sexuality.

Scripture contains explicit commands prohibiting homosexual relations in both the Old and New Testaments.

You are not to sleep with a man as with a woman; it is detestable.
LEVITICUS 18:22

For this reason God delivered them over to disgraceful passions. Their women exchanged natural sexual relations for unnatural ones. The men in the same way also left natural relations with women and were inflamed in their lust for one another. Men committed shameless acts with men and received in their own persons the appropriate penalty of their error.
ROMANS 1:26-27

We know that the law is not meant for a righteous person, but for the lawless and rebellious.
1 TIMOTHY 1:9-10

Concerning homosexuality, the teaching of Scripture is clear. Homosexual relationships are not compatible with God's grander plan for human sexuality. Even so, it is important to remember that discussions about sexuality, even homosexuality, are not primarily about what God prohibits; they are primarily about God's design. We are made to image a holy God, and He has told us how we should live.

IS SAME-SEX ATTRACTION A SPECIAL KIND OF SIN?

Don't you know that the unrighteous will not inherit God's kingdom? Do not be deceived: No sexually immoral people, idolaters, adulterers, or males who have sex with males ... will inherit God's kingdom.
1 CORINTHIANS 6:9-10

We are all broken sexually because of the fall. But because of cultural pressures, it is sometimes tempting for Christians to draw a distinction between homosexuality and other kinds of sins, even other kinds of sexual sins. Scripture doesn't make this distinction. Homosexuality is not a special classification of sin. Yes, the Bible specifically addresses homosexuality, but it also speaks vehemently against sexual immorality of all kinds—including fornication, adultery, and lust. We are all guilty in the category of sexual immorality.

When we're talking to our kids about homosexuality or same-sex attraction we need to use the right vocabulary. There is a significant difference between engaging in a homosexual relationship and struggling with same-sex attraction. In essence, we are talking about the difference between sin and temptation. We have already seen that the Bible condemns homosexuality, but this condemnation is directed toward the practice of homosexuality (e.g. sexual acts or romantic involvement with a person of the same sex). We need to recognize that not every person who is attracted to people of the same sex chooses to act on those desires. There are many Christians who admit to being attracted to people of their same sex who nonetheless agree with the Bible's teaching on homosexuality and seek to flee from this form of sexual sin.

This distinction does not excuse same-sex attraction or make same-sex attraction morally neutral. The Bible portrays any erotic sexual desire apart from the covenant of biblical marriage as falling short of the biblical ideal. Same-sex attraction is still the result of sin and disordered sexual desire, which can lead to lust or further immorality. Yet our message to brothers and sisters who are struggling with same-sex attraction is not one of condemnation, but a message of hope. We call for them to fight against sin

and temptation out of obedience to Jesus. But we do not regard them as a special class of sinners. We are all broken. We all need redemption.

WHAT IF MY CHILD CLAIMS HE IS GAY?

Many Christian parents live with a real fear that one of their children may someday reveal that they experience same-sex attraction. Others have already had a son or daughter admit to being homosexual and did not know how to respond. One of the reasons this is such a crushing experience for many parents is because they assume that their alternatives are limited to affirmation or alienation.

Every child, whether gay or straight, is oriented toward sin, and so are you. If your child or grandchild says he or she is gay, you shouldn't act shocked, as though you are surprised your child might be tempted toward sin, or that you find your own sinful inclinations somehow less deserving of God's judgment.

Your child's point of temptation doesn't mean that your entire relationship with him or her should be defined by that. We never affirm something the Bible says is wrong simply because someone we love is drawn toward it, but that doesn't mean your entire relationship is now to become a sparring match over Romans 1. As a Christian, you believe this person is made in the image of God and thus worthy of love, regardless of how far away from God or from you.

Still, you may be asking, *How do I practically respond to this?* First of all, consider what your child is telling you. He

Jesus isn't shocked by your child's temptations, and He will not leave him alone to fight them.

or she could be saying that this is an identity from which they refuse to repent. That will require a different sort of response than if the child is saying, "This is how I feel, so what do I do?" This will change the way you respond, but what doesn't change is your love and care for this child. Don't panic and don't reject them. Say explicitly that you love that child, no matter what, and mean it. Your relationship wasn't formed by the child's performance, and that won't start now.

If your loved one is a Christian, spend time over the years discipling her about what following Christ looks like. Jesus isn't shocked by your child's temptations, and He will not leave him alone to fight them. The path toward chastity and fidelity to Christ is a difficult one. Your child will need you, the church, and the "large cloud of witnesses" (Heb. 12:1) to cheer her on as she walks a path that can be lonely in a world that too often defines sex and sexuality as ultimate in life.

If your loved one isn't a Christian, express your love, keep the relationship going, and be a gracious gospel witness. God never promises us that our children will all follow Christ. Every wandering son or daughter needs to know that if the moment of crisis comes in his or her life, there's a house waiting with a fatted-calf party ready to go, welcoming the wanderer home (Luke 15:11-32).

God calls parents to love their children. Be clear about your convictions, but do not exile your child from your life. If we sacrifice grace for truth or truth for grace, we will fall short of displaying Christ to others.

LOVE AS JESUS LOVED

Let's be people who respond with grace—not just to our kids, but also to the culture at large. This means we call for repentance inside the church and bear witness to God's pattern for human sexuality outside of the church. Our children will face these issues sooner or later, and we don't want them to face them alone. So let's help our children be prepared for what they will encounter in the world and teach them to love as Jesus loved. After all, what our broken world needs more than anything else is to know the love of Christ.

QUESTIONS FOR REFLECTION

1. Why is it important that we help our child know that all of us are sexually broken?

2. Are you treating homosexuality as a special kind of sin in how you talk about it in front of your children? If so, how can you change that?

3. What's your plan to discuss this issue with your child?

4. How are you helping your child love others as Jesus loved them?

5. What one thing stood out to from this article?

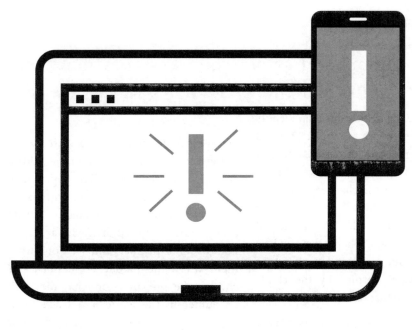

PORNOGRAPHY

For everything in the world—the lust of the flesh, the lust of the eyes, and the pride in one's possessions—is not from the Father, but is from the world.
1 JOHN 2:16

THE PORNOGRAPHY CRISIS

Pornography is perhaps the most destructive moral crisis facing the church today. Christian parents are often unaware of the extent of the threat. In previous generations, access to pornography was limited and it was much easier to safeguard against exposure and consumption. The technology of the modern age has obliterated all barriers to viewing pornography, which has been disastrous for our children.

It is difficult to overstate the extent of the issue. Your sons and daughters will likely be exposed to pornography while they are still children. And not only is it seriously addictive, it is also available on demand through the Internet, to which many children and most teenagers enjoy unrestricted access. As parents, we must protect our children from the snare of pornography.

THE LIE OF ANONYMITY

In a previous era, a person who wanted to consume pornography was forced to declare himself the kind of person who wanted to consume pornography by walking up to a cash register in a convenience store or to a clerk in a video store. Digital technology has spawned an entirely different reality. Thanks to the Internet, any person may now access pornography in secret at any time. The result is a pornography industry that has weaponized itself. As the porn business continues to grow at breakneck speed, in its wake is left a trail of shame, guilt, and broken marriages all over the world.

This will only continue and accelerate. As technology continues to draw itself closer and closer into the human person, the immorality industry will proliferate too. In the future, expect pornography to go beyond being merely visual—it will soon involve all of the senses. Expect the line between pornography and adultery to become murkier and murkier, as our desire to be free from the limits of our flesh ends up exactly where it always does, in the idolatry of the flesh.

Pornography and adultery services are simply new forms of prostitution—a customer paying someone for sex. Our disenchanted sexual age pretends that this is simply a matter of neurology, the manipulation of parts for the purpose of orgasm. The ancient Christian vision, though, tells us something else is going on here. Like the temple prostitution of the Canaanite tribes and the Roman Empire, the prostitution of our time is spiritual to the core. The apostle Paul warned the church at Corinth that the joining of oneself to a prostitute is not merely biological but creates a spiritual reality—joining the body of Christ to a prostitute. This is why the Word of God commands us not just to avoid but also to flee from sexual immorality (1 Cor. 6:12-20).

The brokenness of sexuality all around us demonstrates something far deeper than a crisis of culture. The brokenness of sexuality around us demonstrates a crisis of worship. We will not get out of this with better Internet filters or more accountability groups. We must recognize that technology will continue to offer fallen humanity what it thinks it wants—the illusion that we can transgress God and not surely die. Our only hope starts with the

kind of vision that sees that, no matter the technology, we are never anonymous to God.[4]

WHAT DOES THE BIBLE SAY?

The Bible tells us that God's plan for sexuality is exclusive to the marriage relationship. This was His plan "from the beginning" (Matt. 19:8). God designed human beings to enjoy sexual pleasure, and He intended for that pleasure to take place within the context of the marriage covenant (Gen. 2:24). Satan uses sexual temptation to draw us into sin. He preys upon our good, God-given desires and points them toward sinful ends. And just like Adam and Eve, we are always drawn toward forbidden fruit.

Perhaps a guilty conscience will grasp for a loophole saying that pornography does not violate the one-flesh relationship because it does not involve a physical act with another person. But Jesus stated that, "everyone who looks at a woman lustfully has already committed adultery with her in his heart" (Matt. 5:28). We have all experienced the temptations of lust, and our children will as well, but our hope is found in Jesus:

For we do not have a high priest who is unable to sympathize with our weaknesses, but one who has been tempted in every way as we are, yet without sin. Therefore, let us approach the throne of grace with boldness, so that we may receive mercy and find grace to help us in time of need.
HEBREWS 4:15-16

Jesus, the one who was victorious over all temptation, pleads for us, and the Holy Spirit strengthens us to "stand against the schemes of the devil" (Eph. 6:11). Satan has always used sex to entice and deceive. Peter tells us that false teachers revel "in their deceptions … They have eyes full of adultery that never stop looking for sin. They seduce unstable people and have hearts trained in greed" (2 Pet. 2:14). How many of us have bought into the false promises of immorality peddled by the sex industry? Deception leads us to sin and keeps us there.

A biblical sexual ethic goes beyond simply keeping our bodies in check. Paul instructed us to pursue purity.

Sexual immorality and any impurity or greed should not even be heard of among you, as is proper for saints.
EPHESIANS 5:3

Honoring God with our sexuality means living in purity with our bodies, hearts, minds, and mouths.

THE EFFECTS OF PORNOGRAPHY

When the sexual experience is separated from marriage, it becomes a selfish pursuit.

The gift of sex is given to deepen the bond between a husband and a wife. But the impact (and Satanic aim) of porn is ultimately to dissolve the self-giving nature of sex and empty people's desire for intimacy in marriage.[5]
GARRETT KELL

Consuming pornography is not only wrong, it is harmful. When a person views sexually-explicit material, those images trigger neurons in the brain that stimulate arousal, leading to sexual tension. Pornography produces sinful desires in us and circumvents God's design when sexual expression takes place outside of the marriage covenant.

Pornography trains men to view women as objects—as subjects of his sexual fantasies. Repeated exposure to pornography literally changes the way a man thinks, reducing all women to "potential sexual partners."[6] The more a man gives in to the lure of pornography, the less he is able to enjoy a genuine relationship with a real woman because pornographic pleasure comes easily. The women on the screen always say "yes" and viewing pornography requires none of the patience, love, or discipline of maintaining marital intimacy.

Statistically, less women regularly view pornography than men. However, even for women, that percentage is on the rise. While women are often drawn to pornography for different reasons than men, the effects are just as devastating. Pornography is sought out in order to fill a void or manifest pleasure. It would be foolish to assume that our daughters are immune to this threat. Women are also emotional beings full of sexual desire, and pornography can just as easily affect their abilities to cultivate healthy relationships or enjoy marital intimacy. We need to make sure our churches and our homes are places where wives and daughters can be honest in an appropriate way about their struggles with this particular sin.

Pornography is highly addictive and its effects are truly destructive. It is like a cancer that slowly destroys a person. Not only does pornography harm our ability to relate to others, it creates spiritual problems as well. The danger of pornography is that, like cancer, it eats away at us from the inside. And because it is consumed in secret, it is possible for a person to suffer under the effects of pornography for a long time before it is apparent to those around them. As parents, we must be vigilant to protect our children from the destruction of pornography.

PROTECTING YOUR KIDS

Anticipate that your kids will see pornography and that you will have to deal with this issue. Don't wait to talk about it. Most parents have no idea how early their kids are exposed. You don't want the first conversation to take place when you've already caught him or her in the act.

Establish accountability for everyone in your home. Pornography has no respect for age. Set filters on phones and computers. If filters aren't enough, get rid of Internet-enabled phones. Have all devices out in the open—no TVs, computers, or smartphones behind closed doors.

Don't assume this is only a conversation for boys. Our daughters need the same protection as our sons. Many young girls, just like boys, report seeing their first pornographic image as young as age nine or ten.[7] Often a child's first introduction to pornography is at a friend's house with an image on a phone or computer.

How should you respond if your child is exposed to pornography? Don't overreact. Be calm. Talk about what was seen. Talk about why some people want to look at these images. Acknowledge that the temptation is real and strong, and explain the dignity of the human body and God's design for sexuality. Always make this conversation about the gospel.

Finally, respond with grace. Let confession lead to repentance and repentance to obedience to God's Word. Embrace His promise:

If we confess our sins, he is faithful and righteous to forgive us our sins and to cleanse us from all unrighteousness.
1 JOHN 1:9

QUESTIONS FOR REFLECTION

1. In what ways have you dealt with the temptation of pornography? Has this been a sin problem that you have overcome? If so, how can you pass along what you have learned? If it is still a problem, what steps will you now take to repent and seek help?

2. What protections do you have in place to keep pornography out of your home and out of your child's life?

3. If you've not done so already, what is your plan to discuss this issue with your child?

4. What one thing stood out to you from this article?

BIG IDEA

Provide your child with a strong foundation of godly values and healthy views of sexuality to build upon as they mature.

KEY SCRIPTURES

- *Our bodies belong to God* (1 Cor. 6:19-20).
- *Our bodies are to worship God* (Rom. 12:1-2).
- *Our bodies can be an example to others* (1 Tim. 4:12).
- *Our bodies were created to do good* (Eph. 2:10).

KEY QUESTIONS YOUR PRESCHOOLER IS ASKING

- What is my body for?
- How do I treat my body?
- Why are other bodies different?

AT THIS AGE MOST PRESCHOOLERS WILL …

- Naturally explore their bodies.
- Learn the names for body parts.
- Begin to grasp traits associated with their gender.

DEVELOPMENTAL MILESTONES

- Preschoolers may mindlessly touch their genitals or explore their bodies. This is a natural part of development. Your reaction, including voice tone, word choice, and facial expressions, is one of your child's first lessons in sexuality. Refrain from responding negatively, as this could develop a lifelong association of guilt with his body. Instead, teach your child that a healthy curiosity about his body is a normal part of life.
- Your behavior as a parent is the most influential aspect of developing healthy behaviors. Model healthy ideas of sexuality whenever possible. From your treatment of the opposite sex to your behavior toward nudity, your child will mold her ideas from what you model.
- Kids at this age are incredibly curious, and they often ask tons of questions. Before answering any question on sexuality, clarify what your child is asking, and ask what your child knows about the subject. Then you can better answer your child's specific question. Avoid elaborate detail at this stage, but be truthful and scientific, bringing in God's design for bodies when possible.

COACHING TIPS

- Teach your child that his body is good and has a good purpose to be used like God designed. Try not to respond negatively to any natural curiosity. Instead, redirect any questionable behavior or interest to a healthy alternative.
- Reinforce that you, as the parent, are your child's best resource for questions about her body. Tell your child that she may hear or see things from her friends, but she should always talk to you about questions or ideas she has. Stress the importance of telling you if anything questionable occurs, and give brief examples of such instances. This could include, "Tell me if anyone other than Mommy or Daddy (or other trustworthy adults) touches your private areas," or "Let me know if you ever see anything you think might be wrong." Remember that children are now often exposed to pornography at very early ages.
- Remember that "the talk" is not a singular conversation at a certain age but an ongoing dialogue throughout your child's development. Begin with basic information, like anatomically correct names for body parts, and add age-appropriate information as your child grows. Be aware that your child might be exposed to distorted ideas of sexuality via friends or media, so open communication between parent and child is crucial.

CONVERSATION STARTERS

- **WHY IS THIS OBJECT VALUABLE?** Using a valuable item your child is familiar with, such as a piece of jewelry, illustrate the idea of worth and compare it to our bodies. Explain how the item is special, and because of that, you keep it safe and take good care of it. Point out that it is the same way with our bodies—they are special, so we protect them and take good care of them in the way God made them.
- **WHAT WOULD YOU DO IF ... ?** In order for your child to recognize unsafe or wrong behaviors, role-play possible scenarios as you teach him the proper responses. These situations could include friends or adults trying to cross physical boundaries, like playing "doctor" or offering bribes. Practice saying no, then getting away to tell parents or another trusted adult.
- **WHAT ARE BODIES FOR?** When you and your child encounter expecting or nursing mothers, use the opportunity to discuss how girl and boy bodies each have a different, good purpose from God.

SAY OR PRAY

- God created our bodies.
- God wants us to use our bodies to obey.
- God wants us to take care of our bodies.

BIG IDEA

Provide your children with strong foundations of godly values and healthy views of their bodies and relationships to build upon as they mature.

KEY SCRIPTURES

- *Our bodies belong to God* (1 Cor. 6:19-20).
- *Our bodies are to worship God* (Rom. 12:1-2).
- *Our bodies can be an example to others* (1 Tim. 4:12).
- *Our bodies were created to do good* (Eph. 2:10).

KEY QUESTIONS YOUR ELEMENTARY-AGED CHILD IS ASKING

- How am I supposed to treat my body?
- What is sex?
- Why are bodies different?

AT THIS AGE MOST ELEMENTARY CHILDREN WILL …

- Be increasingly vulnerable to peer pressure.
- Become modest about their bodies.
- Become increasingly concerned with body image.

DEVELOPMENTAL MILESTONES

- Most friendships are still of the same gender at this age, but younger elementary-aged kids will begin mixing and playing with children of the opposite sex.
- They may start showing interest in boy-girl relationships, although they don't like to admit it.

COACHING TIPS

- Expect that your child will have questions about words that they hear related to their bodies. Be ready to answer and explain in language that is age-appropriate, but also clear.
- You can set an example for your child by modeling modesty and a healthy respect for your own body.

- Your child will hear and see things in the media that may not be accurate. This will also happen as they spend time with other kids. Keep the lines of communication open by encouraging him not to be fearful to ask or tell you about anything.
- Discuss private parts and who is allowed to see or touch them. Help your child understand bodily boundaries and encourage her to tell you if anyone tries to cross those boundaries.
- Remember that "the talk" is not a singular conversation at a certain age but an ongoing dialogue throughout your child's development. You want your voice to be heard on this subject before and above the voices of culture, the media, and your child's peers. Take advantage of teachable moments when your child asks questions about anything related to sex and sexuality.

CONVERSATION STARTERS

- **WHAT WOULD YOU DO IF … ?** Lead your child to think about unsafe or wrong situations he might find himself in where he needs to know how to respond quickly. Encourage your child to inform you if he ever finds himself in an unsafe situation.
- **WHAT SHOULD WE EAT TODAY?** As you plan meals or shop at the grocery store, allow your child to help you choose healthy foods. Discuss the importance of eating healthy foods and of taking good care of the bodies God has given us.
- **WHAT ARE YOU WEARING?** Because peer pressure is becoming an issue at this age in a child's life, dressing like "everyone else" may become important to your child. Help your child understand that her body is valuable and should be dressed modestly. Spend time together looking at and evaluating pictures of clothing in magazines or take a shopping trip to look for appropriate clothing.

SAY OR PRAY

- God created our bodies for a purpose.
- Our bodies belong to God.
- We honor God when we use our bodies the way He designed.

BIG IDEA

Provide your preteen with a strong foundation of godly values and healthy views of sexuality to build upon as she matures.

KEY SCRIPTURES

- *Our bodies belong to God* (1 Cor. 6:18-20).
- *Our bodies should be led by the Holy Spirit* (Gal. 5:16-18).
- *Our bodies are created to worship God* (Rom. 12:1-2).
- *Our bodies can be an example to others* (1 Tim. 4:12).
- *Lust is a sin as serious as adultery* (Matt. 5:27-30).
- *Marriage should be an institution between a man and a woman* (Mark 10:6-9).

KEY QUESTIONS YOUR PRETEEN MAY ASK

- Why is my body changing?
- Why am I attracted to this person?
- Is it wrong to feel this way?

AT THIS AGE MOST PRETEENS WILL …

- Be approaching puberty. Girls usually develop ahead of boys.
- Be aware of sex roles and have changing attitudes toward the opposite sex.
- Feel a deep need for the companionship and approval of their peers.
- Hear and discuss topics related to sex.

DEVELOPMENTAL MILESTONES

- As preteens approach and experience puberty, their questions, anxieties, and behaviors concerning sexuality may take on a sense of urgency, embarrassment, or confusion. Be sensitive and understanding as you discuss these issues. As at other childhood stages, be careful about responding negatively.

- A preteen's parents are still the example for attitudes and behavior. Model healthy ideas of sexuality whenever possible. Since your preteen is more capable of abstract thought and analysis, you can be more direct and intentional in your guidance.

- While your preteen may be as curious as a preschooler, she may be less inclined to ask questions. Be proactive in your connecting with your child.

- The majority of boys and girls have been exposed to online pornography by this age.[8] Avoid shaming but be proactive in discussing why pornography is wrong. Put strong safeguards in place to keep pornography out of your home.

• A preteen girl who does not receive words of affirmation and appropriate physical touch from her father or godly male role model may seek to have her needs met through inappropriate verbal and physical expressions of love.

COACHING TIPS

• Tell your child that the body is good and was designed by God for many good purposes. Add that there are also many ways in which people misuse or abuse their bodies that are counter to God's will. Try not to respond negatively to any natural curiosity, as this could build a foundation of shame. Instead, redirect any questionable behavior or interest to a healthy alternative.

• Reinforce that you, as the parent, are your preteen's best and safest resource for questions about sexuality. Affirm often that you are willing to answer any questions or talk about any topic. Stress the importance of telling you if *anything* questionable occurs, especially sexual assault.

• Discussing sexuality is not a singular conversation but an ongoing dialogue as your child develops. You want your voice to be heard on this subject before and above the voices of culture, the media, and your child's peers. Because of intense bodily change and an awakening to physical attraction, your preteen may have questions about the reproductive cycle, masturbation, changes in vocal inflection, and changes in mood and emotion. Open communication between you and your child is critical. Be gentle, honest, and appropriate in your discussions.

CONVERSATION STARTERS

• **IS THERE ANYBODY WHO YOU LIKE OR HAVE A CRUSH ON?** Your preteen may be hesitant to open up with you on this subject, but with careful and gentle communication, this could be a great way to talk about attraction, respect, dating, boundaries, differences between sexes, and God's expectations for our sexuality.

• **WHAT WOULD YOU DO IF ... ?** In order for your child to recognize unsafe or wrong behavior, pose some possible scenarios as you teach your preteen the proper responses to these situations. Reinforce that no means no.

SAY OR PRAY

• God created us in His image, and our bodies have a purpose.
• God wants us to use our bodies the way He designed.
• God tells us there are wrong ways to use our bodies.
• The Bible is full of examples of people who used their sexuality in good or bad ways.

BIG IDEA

Sex should be seen as a good gift created by God to be enjoyed between a man and a woman in the marriage relationship.

KEY SCRIPTURES

- *God created sex as a good gift to be enjoyed between a man and a woman within the marriage relationship* (Gen. 2:8-9,15-25).
- *People can distort and abuse the original design for sex* (Rom. 1:21-28).
- *We are to flee sexual immorality* (1 Cor. 6:12-18).
- *It is God's will that we remain sexually pure* (1 Thess. 4:3-8).
- *Jesus is a friend to sinners and offers forgiveness for those who have sinned sexually* (Luke 5:29-32).

KEY QUESTIONS YOUR MIDDLE SCHOOLER IS ASKING

- Is what's happening to me and what I'm feeling normal?
- What's the truth about sex?
- What should I do and say to impress others?

AT THIS AGE MOST MIDDLE SCHOOLERS WILL …

- Be exposed to things like mature films, sexting, and sexual talk from friends and older siblings. They will also have more unsupervised time online. Therefore, they may be exposed to more information about sex and sexuality than you are aware.
- Navigate the awkwardness of discovering sexuality. They will struggle with what to wear, hairstyles, and other challenges with creating an outward appearance that attracts the opposite sex or strengthens their identity.
- Be going through puberty.

DEVELOPMENTAL MILESTONES

- Lots of physical changes take place as your middle schooler goes through puberty. For boys, the changes include body hair, voice change, and growth spurts. For girls, changes include body shape, body hair, breast development, and the beginning of menstruation.
- With the onset of puberty comes emerging sexuality and sex attraction. Most middle schoolers will begin to turn their attention away from same-gender friendships to relationships with the opposite sex.

- Middle schoolers may begin to compare what they are hearing from the culture about sex with what's being taught to them by parents and other authority figures.

COACHING TIPS

- Most middle schoolers will develop a crush on someone (or several someones) during these years. It might be a celebrity or a friend at school. As a parent make a point to talk about these "loves" in an atmosphere of trust and acceptance. And be ready to listen and help heal the brokenhearted.
- Even though it's hard to believe, you must acknowledge that your child is changing into a young adult, and with that change comes the ability to be involved in sexual relationships. It's imperative that conversations take place about biblical standards for sexuality. They are already hearing lots of inappropriate messages about sex. You need to give them the right ones.
- In your conversations about sex with your middle schooler, it's important that you don't portray the message that sex is bad. Point out Genesis 1–2 where God created everything and called it good, including sexual relations between a man and woman in a covenant relationship of marriage.

CONVERSATION STARTERS

- **DO ANY OF YOUR FRIENDS HAVE BOYFRIENDS/GIRLFRIENDS?** Listen closely to words and body language to gauge true feelings about this situation and also to assess where your middle schooler is when it comes to romantic relationships.
- **WHAT DO YOU THINK GOD THINKS ABOUT SEX?** Don't immediately dismiss your middle schooler's response if it's not quite correct. Move from her responses to share biblical truth.
- **WHAT QUESTIONS DO YOU HAVE ABOUT SEX?** This is the "don't beat around the bush" question. Throw it out there and see how your middle schooler responds. But if and when he ask questions, don't put him off or shuffle him to the other parent. Answer him honestly. You can do this without revealing details not appropriate for middle schoolers.

SAY OR PRAY

- Pray that your middle schooler will understand God's beautiful design for sex and will choose to live by His standards.
- Pray your middle schooler would feel free to ask you any question about sex and that you would have the courage to answer and the wisdom to know what to say.

BIG IDEA

Sex should be seen as a good gift created by God to be enjoyed between a man and a woman in the marriage relationship.

KEY SCRIPTURES

- *God created sex as a good gift to be enjoyed between a man and a woman within the marriage relationship* (Gen. 2:8-9,15-25).
- *People can distort and abuse the original design for sex* (Rom. 1:21-28).
- *We are to flee sexual immorality* (1 Cor. 6:12-18).
- *It is God's will that we remain sexually pure* (1 Thess. 4:3-8).
- *Jesus is a friend to sinners and offers forgiveness for those who have sinned sexually* (Luke 5:29-32).

KEY QUESTIONS YOUR HIGH SCHOOLER IS ASKING

- What's wrong with having sex?
- How far is too far?
- Why is it wrong to be gay?
- Is it right for me to judge others' beliefs about sex?

AT THIS AGE MOST HIGH SCHOOLERS WILL …

- Be establishing their values concerning sexual expression.
- Be trying to clearly define their sexual orientation.
- Have easy access to pornography.
- Face temptation to be sexually active.

DEVELOPMENTAL MILESTONES

- High schoolers are able to critically evaluate what the surrounding culture says about sex and sexuality with what they have been taught by authority figures. Biblical standards will clash with the cultural norms.
- They are physically developed for the most part, especially older high schoolers. Although they may still be growing, they are past the major changes.
- Feelings of love and passion are strong at this age, with a desire to be involved in romantic relationships.

COACHING TIPS

- It's imperative that you discuss sex with your high schooler from a biblical perspective. Champion the positive in that conversation. Point out Genesis 1–2 where God created everything and called it good, including sexual relations between a man and a woman in a covenant relationship of marriage.
- Emphasize that just because her friends may be engaging in sexual activity does not mean she should. Discuss the importance of waiting for God's perfect plan.
- When your high schooler talks with you about sex, don't let your first reaction be shock or condemnation. Yes, discuss God's standards for sex, but a sermon or lecture doesn't need to be the first words out of your mouth.
- Don't assume your high schooler knows what sexual immorality is. Help him know that sexual immorality includes all sexual activity outside of marriage, not just sexual intercourse.
- Statistics prove that almost all high school boys and the majority of high school girls have been exposed to pornography. You must have some frank discussions about the dangers of pornography and your high schooler's involvement. Take needed steps to safeguard your family's access.
- Talking about sex with your high schooler must be an ongoing conversation in your home. Work to create an environment where she can ask or talk to you about anything.

CONVERSATION STARTERS

- **WHAT DO YOU THINK GOD THINKS ABOUT SEX?** You can move this conversation from opinion to the truth about God's standards for sexuality.
- **IS HOMOSEXUALITY A SIN?** This can lead to a multitude of questions about same-sex attraction and sexual orientation. Don't be shocked or panicked if your high schooler reveals he is wrestling with this issue. Be a good listener. Speak biblical truth in love with compassion and grace, reminding him that we all struggle with the temptation to sin.
- **DO YOU THINK PORNOGRAPHY IS A PROBLEM AMONG YOUR FRIENDS?** As noted, there's a good chance your high schooler has, is, or will deal with the sin of pornography. Hopefully this question is a non-threatening way to open a needed discussion.

SAY OR PRAY

- Pray that your high schooler would make wise, godly choices when faced with sexual temptation, and know there is always a way out.
- Pray that your high schooler would feel comfortable in talking with you about anything concerning sexuality.
- Pray that in your own heart and mind you would remain sexually pure and model the biblical standard for sex in your actions and words.

BIG IDEA

Sex should be seen as a good gift created by God to be enjoyed between a man and woman in the marriage relationship.

KEY SCRIPTURES

- *God created sex as a good gift to be enjoyed between a man and a woman within the marriage relationship* (Gen. 2:8-9,15-25).
- *People can distort and abuse the original design for sex* (Rom. 1:21-28).
- *We are to flee sexual immorality* (1 Cor. 6:12-18).
- *It is God's will that we remain sexually pure* (1 Thess. 4:3-8).
- *Jesus is a friend to sinners and offers forgiveness for those who have sinned sexually* (Luke 5:29-32).

KEY QUESTIONS YOUR YOUNG ADULT IS ASKING

- What's wrong with having sex outside of marriage?
- If we are all sinners, how can anyone judge others?
- What's wrong with being gay, lesbian, or transgender?
- How can I love others without endorsing their lifestyle?

AT THIS AGE MOST YOUNG ADULTS WILL …

- Critically evaluate what the surrounding culture says about sex and sexuality with what they have been taught by authority figures.
- Test their beliefs about certain issues including sexuality.
- Engage more in the pursuit of romantic relationships.

DEVELOPMENTAL MILESTONES

- Young adults have more freedom than ever to express themselves sexually. Too often this freedom is translated into casual hook-ups or live-in relationships.
- Students at this age are making plans for their future and relationships are based on individual decisions rather than what others think.
- They have completed their full physical maturation and are usually comfortable with their own body image.
- Students at this age are engaged in higher-level thinking, abstract problem solving, and contrasting culture with Scripture.

COACHING TIPS

- Champion the positive when discussing sex with your young adult. Talk about how God created everything and called it good, including sex. Explain that He has established standards to protect us and provide a life and marriage that flourishes. Discuss the consequences of being sexually active, including how it would affect her relationship with God and a future spouse, her self-confidence, and emotions (shame, guilt).
- Be honest about your own struggles with sexual temptation as a young adult. However, you don't have to be totally transparent to talk about your mistakes and what you learned from them.
- If you find out your young adult has been or is presently sexually active, deal in a redemptive manner with them. Speak the truth in love without condoning or condemning. You want to keep the door open for further conversations. Let your child know that it is never too late to begin making choices about sex that are God honoring.
- Because many young men struggle at some level with pornography, make sure to talk with your son about the dangers of this sin and how to overcome. However, realize that young women can also wrestle with this sin. You may need to have a similar conversation with your daughter.

CONVERSATION STARTERS

- **WHAT MESSAGES DO THE MEDIA AND CURRENT CULTURE PROCLAIM ABOUT SEX?** This question may open a door to discuss the biblical view of sex versus the world's view.
- **IS PORNOGRAPHY A PROBLEM AMONG YOUR FRIENDS?** This may be a non-threatening way to begin a discussion about pornography and your young adult's involvement with it.
- **WHAT IS THE VIEW OF THOSE AROUND YOU CONCERNING HOMOSEXUALITY AND TRANSGENDER ISSUES?** Your young adult is probably hearing lots of differing views and strongly held opinions about these issues. Hopefully this question leads to an honest conversation where you can discuss the biblical view.

SAY OR PRAY

- Pray that God will reveal to your young adult His beautiful design for sex and marriage.
- Pray your young adult will have godly influences around him that point toward a life of purity in Christ.
- Pray for your young adult's future spouse. Pray for God to protect that person and shape that future mate into the person He desires.

SESSION 5

RELATIONSHIPS

GUIDING THROUGH FRIENDSHIPS, ROMANCE, AND BROKEN HEARTS

Use the space below to record notes, quotes, thoughts, and questions from the video panel discussion.

_____

_____

_____

_____

_____

_____

_____

_____

_____

_____

_____

_____

_____

_____

_____

_____

_____

_____

_____

_____

_____

_____

_____

_____

GROUP GUIDE

Use the following questions and prompts to continue the conversation about the issues discussed by the video panel.

What are your children learning about marriage from your marriage?

How many of you know families that have gone through divorce? How many of you know single-parent families? How many know families with same-sex parents? How are you talking about these households with your children?

Do you ever speak of divorce as a sin? If not, why not? Is it important that we do? Why or why not?

For those of you who have experienced divorce, how did you handle it with your children, both positively and negatively?

How much should you as a parent speak into your child's friendships? How can you help your child build lasting friendships?

What is your approach with your child on dating? How is it different than when you were growing up?

Does your child know you and your spouse's dating/courtship story? How is sharing it with him or her helpful?

How can you help your child walk through break-ups and friendship dissolutions?

Does your child have grandparents close by? Why is that important? If grandparents aren't physically close, how can you surround your child with grandparent-type people?

David Prince talked about shaping our children to be intentional in reaching out to people who are marked with all kinds of "otherness." Why is this important? How is this happening in your home?

Do you consider your family as evangelists? Why should you? How do you foster that identity in your family?

TAKEAWAYS:

A PICTURE OF MARRIAGE

David Platt says, "The purpose of marriage is for the display of the gospel and a demonstration of the glory of our God."[1]

Our picture of marriage is broken. We know that marriage is meant to be a picture of the gospel, but sadly, many of the marriages that we see each day bear the marks of sin and brokenness. In our culture, marriage is seldom associated with selfless, redemptive love. And if marriage is distorted, so is the gospel. That is why now, perhaps more than ever, it is critical that we recover a biblical view of marriage.

WHAT DOES THE BIBLE SAY?

Marriage is not a product of society. Marriage was God's idea. He created it. From the very beginning, God's Word clearly teaches God's design for the union of man and woman. Scripture starts with a marriage as Adam and Eve are united as "one flesh" (Gen. 2:24) and ends with a wedding feast as Jesus is joined to his bride (Rev. 19:6-10).[2]

Throughout history, from the garden of Eden to the marriage supper of the Lamb, marriage endures.

God's ideal for marriage is the union of one man and one woman for one lifetime. Jesus affirmed this in Matthew 19 saying,

"Haven't you read," he replied, "that he who created them in the beginning made them male and female," and he also said, "For this reason a man will leave his father and mother and be joined to his wife, and the two will become one flesh? So they are no longer two, but one flesh. Therefore, what God has joined together, let no one separate."
MATTHEW 19:4-6

Marriage doesn't begin with you and your happiness. Marriage begins with God. He gave us marriage. And we need to understand His plan.

THE PURPOSE OF MARRIAGE

Today, marriage is seen as unnecessary and optional. Culture argues that the desirable benefits of marriage (sex and companionship) can easily be obtained in other ways. "Marriage" is nothing more than a piece of paper, or worse a matter of convenience—something to stick with until it becomes a burden or until a better opportunity presents itself.

It is common for young people to see marriage and family as obstacles to personal goals and career advancement. Others embrace marriage as a means for emotional fulfillment, a cure for loneliness, or an outlet for romantic desire. But all of this underestimates the value and purpose of marriage.

Marriage doesn't begin with you and your happiness. Marriage begins with God. He gave us marriage. And we need to understand His plan.

A MARRIAGE BLUEPRINT

Let's begin with a definition. *Marriage* is a gift from God that reflects the gospel in our most intimate relationship in a way that demonstrates God's love and enables us to become more like Jesus.

We should always think of marriage as sacred, permanent, and exclusive. It is sacred because it is a gift of God. It is permanent because it is a covenant intended to last a lifetime. And it is exclusive because it is limited in nature and expression to one man and one woman.

Marriage also has essential benefits. Through marriage, we experience intimate companionship within a lifelong covenant. Through marriage, we experience the biblical blueprint for sexual expression and fulfillment. Through marriage, a husband and wife may produce children.

In Genesis 1:28, the first command in Scripture, God said, "Be fruitful, multiply, fill the earth, and subdue it …" The sexual union of husband and wife is not only meant for pleasure, it is also the biblical means for the continuation of society. And because marriage was God's idea, it should not surprise us that it is uniquely suited for human flourishing. This can be seen in several rather obvious ways.

Consider that man and woman are designed to complement one another—both in anatomy and in terms of responsibility. Not only does the sexual union of man and woman result in offspring, but God also designed men and women to fulfill distinct roles in the family (e.g. protecting and nurturing). As a permanent union, the marriage covenant "brings stability to the relationship" and "provides a strong incentive to sacrifice, forgive, and seek the best interest of one's spouse."[3] Healthy marriages serve the physical and emotional needs of spouses and children, and reflect the goodness of the gospel.

THE WHOLE BODY OF CHRIST

Lifting up marriage as the foundation for human flourishing should not exclude non-married people or single parents from the conversation. Marriage is not only for the edification of the married couple. God gave us marriage to be a visible object lesson to teach us about who He is and who we are in relationship to Him.[4]

Through marriage, you model love, forgiveness, and service for the whole church body. Singles observe sacrificial love in the marriage relationship and see an image of our Savior who humbly gave Himself for us. Your children watch as you work out conflict with patience and faithfulness, and they come to better understand the long-suffering of God with us. For the single parent who is reading this, and reads that it is God's plan for children to have a mom and a dad who are joined together in a permanent, covenant relationship: You are not lessened in your singleness. No one "parents" alone. Sam Allberry said, "If it takes a village to raise a child, it takes a church to raise a Christian."[5]

"Mothering" is not only for mothers. It is the responsibility of every woman in the church to be fruitful and multiply, not only biologically, but also spiritually. All of us are mothering and fathering, even if we're single, or married without kids. As people who are living together in community, your children have the distinct opportunity of having spiritual mothers and fathers in the church. Where you are weak, another may be strong. Where you lack courage, another may be brave. This is so much more than who is driving the carpool this week. We need spiritual mothers and fathers in the church because there is wisdom in many counselors.

Is there someone you need to reach out to in your church body? Are there men and women in your spiritual community who would gladly and humbly support you in your goal of Christ-centered parenting? Is there someone whom you need to come alongside? Do not be afraid, God expects His people to help and care for one another.

CHRIST AND HIS BRIDE

We have seen that marriage is meant to be complementary, exclusive, and permanent. We have seen that marriage is the foundation for human flourishing. But we could embrace all of these things and still miss the most significant thing about marriage. Marriage is meant to display the love of Christ for His bride, the church.

In Ephesians 5, Paul spelled out roles for husbands and wives and then looked back to Genesis 2 to say about the one-flesh union, "This mystery is profound, but I am talking about Christ and the church." Our marriages reflect the gospel to an unbelieving world. When husbands love their wives "just as Christ loved the church" (Eph. 5:25) the world sees a picture of a Savior who loved us so much He went to the cross for us. When wives submit joyfully in marriage, the world sees what it means to joyfully serve the Lord (Eph. 5:24).

We have a lot of broken pictures, making it much messier than God intended. But even so, "the unique relationship between man and woman joined together in marriage is the closest approximation we have of how much God loves us, and a picture of his plan to be with us forever."[6] This is why we must strive to faithfully embody the biblical picture of marriage—we must show the world a better picture of Jesus.

A GOSPEL LEGACY

God uses marriage to teach us many things. Marriage is permanent because God's love for His people is never-ending. Marriage is exclusive because we are to put nothing else above or before God. Marriage is complementary because we are not self-sufficient, but Christ is sufficient for all our needs—He is the only One who satisfies our deepest longings. Every aspect of marriage was designed to illuminate the relationship between God and His people.[7]

Just because you have an imperfect marriage history does not mean you can't present a biblical view of marriage to your kids. The Bible is full of sordid examples of imperfect families—Abraham the liar, Jacob the manipulator, David the adulterer and murderer, Rahab the prostitute (and great-great-grandmother of King David), and many others. God knows we make mistakes. He gave us feeble, human examples in Scripture so we would know we're not alone. So whether you are enjoying a healthy marriage, living as a single parent, or you are a child who has never experienced God's design for families, there is hope and grace for you. More than anything else, marriage points us to the love and grace of God available to us in the gospel. Wherever you are in life, your imperfections don't disqualify you from modeling the love of Christ as best you can.

Parents, we can't just tell our kids what marriage is; we must live it out for them to see. You have the opportunity, no matter how imperfectly, to model repentance, forgiveness, unity, self-control, joy, giving, thankfulness, love, perseverance, and patience. Do your kids see genuine love between you and your spouse? Do they see the gospel in your marriage? Your child observes plenty of marriages on a daily basis. Let yours be the one he or she wants to model.

QUESTIONS FOR REFLECTION

1. How would you have defined marriage before reading this article?

2. How has your view of marriage changed?

3. Is your marriage currently reflecting the gospel? Why or why not?

4. How are you mothering and fathering people in the body of Christ?

5. What one thing stood out to you from this article?

MARRIAGE & BROKENNESS

Marriage is to be honored by all and the marriage bed kept undefiled, because God will judge the sexually immoral and adulterers.
HEBREWS 13:4

Marriage is an institution that points to the gospel. God created marriage to teach us about His love. But, as we have seen, reality often falls short of this ideal. And sadly, our kids are growing up in a world where marriage serves as one more tragic reminder of the good life we lost in the garden of Eden.

As parents, it is our job to help our kids see the truth about marriage. One of our greatest challenges will be equipping them to understand the various ways that marriage is distorted in our culture. Even so, as we confront these difficult realities both in conversation and in our daily lives, our goal is to train our children to see broken marriages the same way they should see all the effects of the fall—through the redemptive lens of the gospel.

COHABITATION

If marriage is good for human flourishing, why are so many young adults choosing to delay marriage? In 2014, almost half of all adults ages twenty-five to thirty-four had never married, up from only twelve percent in 1960.[8] Though there are multiple contributing factors, among the most alarming reasons for this statistic is the rise of cohabitation—two adults living together and having a sexual relationship without being married. Today, roughly a quarter of adults ages twenty-five to thirty-four who have never been married are living with a partner.[9] And not only that, but the number of adults cohabiting and raising children outside of marriage is also on the rise.

Cohabitation distorts the gospel. A man and a woman simply living together in the same house does not represent the image of Christ's covenantal, sacrificial, eternal relationship to His bride that God intended. Marriage is a covenant union and the practice of cohabitation is a cheap imitation—everything about it screams "temporary."

Let's be clear about something: marriage is God's idea, and we are not free to alter His design. Cohabitation seeks to enjoy the benefits of marriage while avoiding the responsibilities of marriage. It is a dangerous formula and it is rooted in sin. Help your child understand why cohabitation conflicts with God's design for marriage.

DIVORCE

Divorce has become commonplace in our society. Our legal system is partially to blame. Before the introduction of no-fault divorce laws in the 1970s, married couples needed a specific reason for courts to grant a divorce, such as adultery, abuse, or neglect. But with the advent of these laws, divorce became an option under any circumstance and the divorce rate steadily began to rise.[11]

But this doesn't explain *why* marriage doesn't work for so many people. That is a difficult question, one we are not prepared to answer on behalf of society at large, but we can discuss some of the reasons that so many Christians have turned to divorce. On a very basic level, we've forgotten what marriage is. We have made marriage about us (our happiness, desires, and plans) and not about the gospel and the glory of God. We have become very pragmatic when it comes to marriage—adopting an attitude that says

We want our kids to believe that marriage is sacred and permanent, but we also want them to know that God can redeem any situation.

"I'm in as long as this works for me." This is not the way of our Savior who "humbled himself by becoming obedient to the point of death—even to death on a cross" (Phil. 2:8). A divorce culture happens when we forget about the gospel and treat marriage like a contract, rather than a covenant; contracts expire, covenants last forever.

Divorce will be a reality for your kids. Even if they enjoy the benefits of a happy two-parent home, they will experience broken marriages through relatives and friends. Help them understand how divorce distorts God's design for marriage while teaching them to view the broken marriages they see through the lens of the gospel. We want our kids to believe that marriage is sacred and permanent, but we also want them to know that God can redeem any situation.

SAME-SEX MARRIAGE

On June 26, 2015, the United States Supreme Court ruled that same-sex couples possess a constitutional right to marry, legalizing same-sex marriage in all fifty states. Before and after that decision, we have seen the media attempt to normalize same-sex marriage as much as possible by including same-sex couples in TV shows, commercials, and magazines. This is the new normal. From this point forward, our children will grow up with this reality. How do you address this issue with your kids?

First of all, make no mistake: you should talk to your children about this. The Bible isn't nearly as antiseptic as Christians sometimes pretend to be, and it certainly doesn't shirk back from addressing all the complexities of human life. If we are discipling our children, let's apply the Scriptures to all of life. If we refuse to talk to our children about the reality of the world they live in, our children will assume we are unequipped to speak to it, and they'll eventually search out a worldview that will.

This doesn't mean that we rattle our children with information they aren't developmentally ready to process. For instance, when we talk about marriage, we give age-appropriate answers to the "Where do babies come from?" question. There is no need to inform small children in graphic detail about all the sexual possibilities in order to get across that Jesus calls us to live as husbands and wives with fidelity, permanence, and complementarity.

Some parents believe that teaching their children the controversies about same-sex marriage will promote homosexuality, but sexual orientation doesn't work that way. In fact, the exact opposite is true. If you don't teach your children about God's plan for human sexuality, the ambient culture—which is now codified in our legal system—will fill in your silence with answers of its own.

You can explain to your children what the Bible teaches—from Genesis to Jesus to the apostles—about a man and a woman becoming one flesh. You can explain that as Christians we believe this marital relationship is different than other relationships we have. And yes, you can then tell them that some people have relationships they want to be seen as marriages, and that the Supreme Court agreed with them, but that we as Christians cannot.

Instead of avoiding the subject, consider it an important opportunity to instruct your children in the Lord. Explain to them that you love your neighbors who disagree with you on this. Explain that all people ought to be free from mistreatment or harassment. And then explain that the church believes government can't actually define or redefine marriage at all. Government can only recognize what God created and placed in creation. Far from doing harm, these conversations provide avenues for your children to learn why you think mothers and fathers are different, and why those differences are good.

As you discuss these things, look for examples in your own family of how those differences work together for the good of the household, and point to examples in Scripture of the same.

Don't ridicule or express hostility toward those who disagree. Don't give in to panic or rage about the country. You might have gay or lesbian family members; be sure to express your love for them to your children, even as you say that you disagree about God's design for marriage. You probably have already had to do that with family members or friends who are divorced, cohabiting, or some other

Your success as a parent is measured by your faithfulness to God's design for parenting.

situation that falls short of a Christian sexual ethic. If your children see outrage in you, rather than a measured and Christlike biblical conviction, they eventually will classify your convictions here in the same category as your clueless opinions about "kids these days and their loud music."

The issues at stake are more important than that. Marriage isn't ultimately about living arrangements or political structures, it's about the gospel.[12]

HOW DO WE RESPOND?

Step lightly with these issues. Do your best to help your kids see the purpose of God's design for marriage. Show grace to them as they ask questions about how to live out a biblical conviction in a culture that opposes God's truth.

These are not easy things to grasp. In fact, your child may not agree with your views on cohabitation, divorce, or homosexuality. They may even embrace one of these sinful paths. In any case, don't panic. Remember the story of the prodigal son (Luke 15). The son left home, squandered his father's money, and slandered his character. But when the son realized his own foolishness, he knew he had a family to go home to. As you discuss or encounter these subjects, make sure your children know how much you love them. As much as possible, keep the door of peace open to your kids. God is patient with you, so be patient with them.[13]

If possible, as far as it depends on you, live at peace with everyone.
ROMANS 12:18

One of the most important things to remember is that your success as a parent is not determined by your ability to raise perfect children. Your success as a parent is measured by your faithfulness to God's design for parenting. You yourself may have previously embraced some of these sinful patterns. Remember that the gospel is a message of grace and redemption. We will never measure up. That is why the gospel is good news. Because of Jesus, God will make beautiful things out of our brokenness.

QUESTIONS FOR REFLECTION

1. How are you currently helping your child deal with the cultural distortions of marriage?

2. Have you talked with your child about the reality of same-sex marriage? Why or why not? Why is it important that you do?

3. How are you as a family loving and showing grace to those who are living outside the biblical view of marriage?

4. What one thing stood out to you from this article?

DATING AND SINGLE- NESS

For this is God's will, your sanctification: that you keep away from sexual immorality, that each of you knows how to control his own body in holiness and honor, not with lustful passions, like the Gentiles, who don't know God.
1 THESSALONIANS 4:3-5

In the church, we often speak about God's pattern for marriage and sexuality, but it is less common to hear discussions about dating and singleness. This is a real problem because our kids are receiving very clear instructions about both dating and singleness every day. The culture's approach to dating is antithetical to the Bible's view of marriage. Instead of promoting selfless love and lifelong commitment, the culture says dating is about self-fulfillment and exploration. And instead of esteeming marriage as a source of true satisfaction, the culture encourages singles to delay marriage as long as possible in order to maximize independence and freedom. How can we possibly expect our kids to embrace a biblical view of marriage unless we are committed to helping them?

Let's begin with some parameters. We understand that individual families will approach dating in different ways. Our goal is to offer you a biblical, concrete foundation to build upon as you and your family approach these issues.

WHAT DOES THE BIBLE SAY?

The Bible includes a clear biblical sexual ethic for non-married people. We know that sexual intimacy is reserved for a man and woman who are united together through the marriage covenant (Gen. 2:24). But one of the reasons that Christians have a difficult time with the subject of dating is because the Bible has no such category. Dating is a convention of the modern age. Before dating was around, a man would simply "pursue a woman toward marriage."[14]

In many ways, dating imitates marriage. Like marriage, dating is based on two people cultivating romantic and emotional bonds in the context of commitment. But unlike marriage, dating relationships are temporal by nature. Dating fosters dependence and sexual intimacy, but it lacks the protective measures of the marriage covenant. Even so, dating has become a fixed practice in our culture and we must learn how to approach it as Christians.

For the Christian, if the only thing that changes when you get married is that you start having sex, something is wrong with the picture. When we read the common thread of Scripture, from Genesis to Jesus to Paul, we read that, "a man will leave his father and mother and be joined to his wife, and the two will become one flesh ... so they are no longer two, but one flesh" (Matt. 19:5-6).[15]
DEAN INSERRA

This should lead Christians to take a different approach to dating. While, it is fine to evaluate whether two people are compatible before setting a wedding date, a Christian approach to dating stops far short of "giving ourselves away emotionally, romantically, and sexually to someone who is not our husband or wife."[16] Dating relationships are not permanent—none of them are. Too often we justify unhealthy dating practices because two people might or are planning to get married. Nothing is marriage but marriage (Heb. 13:4). The Bible tells us not to "stir up or awaken love until the appropriate time" because marital love is dangerous apart from the marriage covenant (Song of Sol. 2:7). We should be careful not to embrace a view of dating that actually describes marriage.

WHAT DOES IT MEAN TO GUARD YOUR HEART?

"Guard your heart" is a common piece of advice in Christian circles. It comes from the Book of Proverbs:

Guard your heart above all else,
for it is the source of life.
PROVERBS 4:23

But what does it mean to guard your heart? And how do you do it? Paul says,

Don't worry about anything, but in everything, through prayer and petition with thanksgiving, present your requests to God. And the peace of God, which surpasses all understanding, will guard your hearts and minds in Christ Jesus.
PHILIPPIANS 4:6-7

This has particular application for marriage and singleness. Paul tells us that prayer is the pathway to guarding our hearts and minds with the peace of God.

Guarding your heart begins with prayer to God and overflows into communication with the other person. In other words, the key to guarding your heart is to talk to God about the relationship before you talk to the other person about the relationship. This will help keep things in proper perspective.

There is real danger in failing to do this. First, if you fail to guard your heart, you may move too fast in the relationship, becoming too vulnerable too quickly. Second, you may

The heart refers to who you are as a person and the Bible is teaching you to guard yourself. Take care to live and walk before God in ways that are pleasing to Him.

fail to seek God's desires for the relationship by depending on your own understanding and priorities (Prov. 3:5-6).

Why do you guard your heart? We learn from the Old Testament that our hearts are vulnerable (Jer. 17:9) and easily drawn into sin (Gen. 6:5). While we often view the heart as the seat of our emotions and our will, yet Israel understood the heart to be the center of the whole person—not just our emotions and will but also of wisdom and perspective.

The heart refers to who you are as a person and the Bible is teaching you to guard yourself. Take care to live and walk before God in ways that are pleasing to Him.

May the words of my mouth and the meditation of my heart be acceptable
to you, LORD, my rock and my Redeemer.
PSALM 19:14

Look back at Proverbs 4:23. It instructs to you to "guard the heart" (who you are) because "it is the source of life" (what you do flows from it). When it comes to dating, it is essential for you to guard your heart because what you do in a dating relationship flows from who you are in a dating relationship. We often treat the idea of guarding your heart as if it merely involves protecting yourself from too much intimacy with someone of the opposite sex. Certainly this is necessary, but guarding your heart is so much more than this! It's a call to protect your character in all that you do.

A WORD ABOUT SINGLENESS

The Bible exhorts us to honor marriage in our churches, and rightfully so, as it is a portrait of God's love for us. But let's be clear: A person is not less than whole if he or she is not married or in a dating relationship. In fact, the Bible tells us that those who remain unmarried are able to "be devoted to the Lord without distraction" (1 Cor. 7:35). Consider Jesus, whose personhood is not diminished in the least because He is single. Additionally, singleness does not mean being alone. The body of Christ is the family of God, and every Christian—single or otherwise—is a member of this spiritual family (Rom. 8:14).

For those seeking marriage, remember that we trust in a sovereign God who is more than able to bring two people together. Instead of casually "dating around," earnestly pray and ask the Lord for a husband or wife. As you develop healthy, meaningful friendships with Christians of the opposite sex, seek to identify the qualities you desire in a future spouse. Christians should approach marriage carefully. There are dangers on both sides—in moving too quickly or in delaying marriage for too long. In seeking out a spouse, our strong encouragement is to prioritize his or her commitment to Jesus and the church. As you evaluate

the possibility of a certain man or woman, trust the advice of godly counsel and allow multiple people to affirm any decision to move forward (Prov. 11:14).

INTENTIONAL DATING

Christians should not follow the culture's lead on the issue of dating. We encourage each family to tailor their approach in ways that work for them. In light of that, we offer some general guidance from a gospel-shaped framework to dating.

First, the purpose of dating is to find a spouse. A lot of times, kids begin pursuing dating relationships prematurely simply because everyone else seems to be doing the same thing. Make sure you are the one shaping your child's thoughts about dating and guide them to seek out a dating relationship at the appropriate time.

As you approach this conversation, consider these questions: At what age will you allow your child to date? Will he or she only go on group dates, date alone, or date with a chaperone? How much time will he or she spend with a boyfriend or girlfriend?

Set clear expectations. Let your child know that you will talk to a potential boyfriend or girlfriend and have a conversation with his or her parents before your son or daughter goes on a date.

Be on the lookout for unhealthy behaviors. Look for signs of growing emotional dependence and physical intimacy. Don't be afraid to step in if the relationship has become harmful.

Help your children pursue the right goals. As they begin to date, teach them to live with integrity and pursue Christlike holiness. Teach them to glorify God with their bodies and emotions. And teach them to honor their future spouse in the way that they conduct themselves.

FINAL THOUGHTS

Every child will eventually face questions about dating and singleness. For Christian parents, we want our kids to approach these issues with biblical wisdom, with the goal of honoring God with their emotions, bodies, and lives. The best way for our children to remain faithful to Jesus is for us to commit to guide them each step of the way.

QUESTIONS FOR REFLECTION

1. What's the current conversation about dating in your home?

2. How are you helping your child move toward a biblical view of dating and marriage?

3. What does it mean to guard your heart? How are you helping your child understand this important concept?

4. What one thing stood out to you from this article?

BIG IDEA

Provide your child a healthy concept of friendships, marriage, and other relationships in a society that constantly diminishes the value of these connections.

KEY SCRIPTURES

- *We are to love God and love others* (Luke 10:27).
- *We need relationships to help us* (Ecc. 4:9-12).
- *We are to keep peace with each other* (Eph. 4:1-3).
- *We are to serve others* (Phil. 2:3).
- *God gives us marriage* (Gen. 2:24).

KEY QUESTIONS YOUR PRESCHOOLER IS ASKING

- Why do people get married?
- Who can get married?
- How do we treat people?

AT THIS AGE MOST PRESCHOOLERS WILL …

- Begin to recognize different types of relationships.
- Begin to understand the right ways and wrong ways to treat people.
- Group themselves based on gender.

DEVELOPMENTAL MILESTONES

- Preschoolers don't fully understand the concept of marriage, so they often have erroneous ideas, like "When I get older, I'm going to marry my mommy." Never respond in shock or disapproval to these types of statements—simply explain the truth.
- Children at this age often have "boyfriends" or "girlfriends" at school or church. Remember that preschoolers do not understand these relationships as adults do. It is best to respond neutrally to this information, not encouraging the behavior but not conveying distress about it either.
- At this stage, the most important relationships outside of the family are your child's peers. Stress often the importance of showing respect to others and including everyone. Encourage your child to reach out to new playmates. Teach them relational skills and how to connect with others.

COACHING TIPS

- Parents are the most effective example of a healthy relationship. Modeling respectful and loving relationship behavior with your spouse is of the utmost importance. How a child's parents communicate affects him, so explaining and modeling healthy ways to solve disagreements is important. Also showing him that marriage takes commitment and work will paint a more realistic picture.
- In addition to modeling healthy relationship behavior, draw attention to unhealthy relationship behavior as well. Reinforce good decisions in relationships and give examples of negative relationship choices, such as "Hitting or saying mean things to each other is never OK in a relationship" or "God planned for families to love one another." Other important topics to discuss might include appropriate versus inappropriate touch.
- Although preschoolers are too young to understand the metaphor of marriage as Christ and His bride, it is never too early to observe and discuss biblical relationships, both marriages and friendships. These examples can shape a sense of respect for others, building a firm foundation for healthy relationships in the future.

CONVERSATION STARTERS

- **WHAT DO YOU THINK MOMMY AND DADDY'S WEDDING LOOKED LIKE?** Begin the discussion on healthy relationships early. As they grow, add more information and details on the subject according to their age and understanding. Looking at wedding pictures, reading children's books, or even examining relationships in children's movies can be good starting places to open the discussion.
- **HOW DO YOU KNOW?** Ask your child how she knows her dad loves her mom or how she knows her grandparents love each other. Not only does this give you a glimpse into your child's mind, but it can open a dialogue about traits of a loving relationship or allow you opportunities to clarify any misconceptions.
- **WHAT DOES GOD SAY?** Starting with small, concrete examples, have a conversation with your child about some of God's truths. Mention that sometimes the world says things that go against God's truths, like what marriage is. Talk about the story of Adam and Eve as God's first example of marriage.

SAY OR PRAY

- God created Adam and Eve. They were the first husband and wife.
- God created humans to have relationships.
- God wants us to love others.
- God created people so we wouldn't be lonely.

BIG IDEA

Provide your child a healthy concept of friendships, marriage, and other relationships in a society that constantly diminishes the value of these connections.

KEY SCRIPTURES

- *We are to love God and love others* (Luke 10:27).
- *We need relationships to help us* (Ecc. 4:9-12).
- *We are to keep peace with each other* (Eph. 4:1-3).
- *We are to serve others* (Phil. 2:3).
- *God gives us marriage* (Gen. 2:24).

KEY QUESTIONS YOUR ELEMENTARY-AGED CHILD IS ASKING

- Why do people get married?
- What's wrong with same-sex marriage?
- How should we treat other people?

AT THIS AGE MOST ELEMENTARY CHILDREN WILL ...

- Befriend children of the opposite gender but prefer peers of the same sex.
- Begin to think more about the future.
- Possibly start showing interest in girl-boy relationships.

DEVELOPMENTAL MILESTONES

- Younger elementary age children are beginning to develop a conscience and to test values. They will be exposed to values that are contrary to what the Bible teaches. Guide your child toward biblical truths as questions about friendships, relationships, and marriage arise.
- Children at this age are developing concepts of love and trust. Help your child understand these concepts not only by teaching biblical principles but also by modeling love and trust for her.
- Children at this age are eager to please and want to be liked by peers and adults. Reinforce the importance of treating other people in ways that will please God.

COACHING TIPS

- Discuss what the Bible says about marriage. Explain that in a healthy marriage, a man and a woman keep the promises they made to God and each other to love and stay committed to each other through good and bad times. Point out that although God's desire is for marriage to last until death, sometimes things happen that cause couples to separate (divorce), but God still loves them.

- Your child will likely hear about or witness relationships that are not in agreement with what the Bible teaches. Lead him to understand what God says about these relationships. Explain that God's plan is always the best plan. Tell your child that although some people choose to live in ways not pleasing to God, He still loves them.

- Help your child learn positive ways to handle conflict in relationships. Be a good example of conflict resolution in the relationships in your own life. Be aware of ways your child handles conflict, and guide her to make changes as needed. Offer praise when you see her solving disagreements in positive ways.

CONVERSATION STARTERS

- **DO YOU KNOW WHY MOM AND DAD GOT MARRIED?** Start a conversation about marriage by talking about your marriage. Talk about how you met, your dating experiences, why you decided to get married, and so forth. Address the challenges of marriage and how you and your spouse deal with those challenges. For fun, look at your wedding pictures with your child.

- **WHO IS YOUR BEST FRIEND?** As your child talks about her friends, ask questions like "How do you know she's your friend?," "How do you show your friend you like him?," or "Is there someone you know who needs a friend?" Use this opportunity to discuss how to treat others in ways that please God.

- **WHAT WOULD YOU DO IF …?** Lead your child through role-playing exercises dealing with conflict situations she may encounter (or has already encountered). Consider situations she might face at home, school, with friends, and so forth. By anticipating situations and preparing to respond in God-pleasing ways, she will learn techniques she can carry into adulthood.

SAY OR PRAY

- God created marriage with Adam and Eve.
- Marriage is a promise between a man and a woman to love and stay committed to one another through good and bad times.
- God wants us to love Him and other people.
- God wants us to have good and appropriate relationships with other people.

BIG IDEA

Provide your preteen a healthy concept of friendships, marriage, and other relationships in a society that constantly diminishes the value of these connections.

KEY SCRIPTURES

- *We are called to have close friendships* (Prov. 18:24).
- *We are to have healthy, supportive relationships* (Ecc. 4:9-12).
- *We must love God, and we must love others* (Luke 10:27).
- *We should keep peace with one another* (Eph. 4:2-3).
- *We are to serve others* (Phil. 2:3).
- *Marriage is a symbolic Christlike union between a man and a woman* (Eph. 5:25-33).

KEY QUESTIONS YOUR PRETEEN MAY ASK

- Will I get married some day? When? How will I know who's the right person?
- How should I deal with people who are mean to me?
- What is it like to have a boyfriend/girlfriend?

AT THIS AGE MOST PRETEENS WILL …

- Have formed concepts of personal worth.
- Have developed a conscience and a value system.
- Be capable of deep, complex relationships with peers.
- Find themselves attracted to members of the opposite sex.

DEVELOPMENTAL MILESTONES

- Preteens will have a richer understanding of the concept of marriage and may entertain serious (but still immature) considerations about the realities of married life. They also will be aware of divorce and same-sex marriage, though they may not totally comprehend the implications and consequences of these issues.
- Your preteen may feel ready for or actually enter into a more "romantic" relationship. Because of the influence of his peers and the different boundaries of other parents, it's important to fully explain your boundaries, values, and views.
- As your preteen develops friendships with like-minded peers, she will find more pronounced dissimilarities with certain people (ideological, interest-based, jealousy-induced, or otherwise). Some preteens may develop "rivals." Be ready to help her navigate possible conflicts and to disarm possible resentments that may surface between your child and her peers.

- The role of digital communication and social media in friendships and boyfriend/girlfriend relationships is pervasive. Being aware is crucial. Set limits but also explain with grace your hope for fully-developed healthy relationships.

COACHING TIPS

- Model respectful and loving behavior with your spouse. Your communication with one another will affect your child in subtle and overt ways. Explaining ways that people solve disagreements or approach commitment will help present a realistic viewpoint.
- While modeling a healthy relationship, also discuss unhealthy or negative relationship behaviors. Topics to discuss could include domestic violence, inappropriate touching, premarital sex and/or cohabitation, and same-sex marriage. Help your child know how to identify these relationships and how to respond to them graciously and without harsh judgment.
- Compare biblical standards for marriages, friendships, and other relationships with the world's standards. Explain why and how they should live with godly values in their relationships.
- Be invested in your preteen's social and extracurricular life. Some may become discouraged when they see peers entering into relationships as they remain single. Talk with your child about singleness, loneliness, and the often unrealistic expectations that individuals invest into their significant others.

CONVERSATION STARTERS

- **WHY DO YOU AND [ONE OF YOUR PRETEEN'S FRIENDS] GET ALONG?** This question will require your preteen to think critically about the tenets of a positive relationship. Use this conversation as a way to steer your child toward new ways of examining what makes for sustainable friendships. A counter-question might be, *Why don't you and so-and-so get along?*
- **WHAT DOES GOD SAY?** Starting with small, concrete examples, talk with your preteen about biblical truths. Discuss how the world glorifies things that go against God's will, such as same-sex marriage. Make sure the truth is clear, but emphasize we are not to ostracize or condemn those who think differently. Explain that we are to love all people as Jesus did.

SAY OR PRAY

- God created humans to form a relationship with Him through Christ.
- God created humans to form loving relationships with others.
- God does not want us to be lonely.
- God wants us to be peaceful with our neighbor.
- God created marriage with Adam and Eve.

BIG IDEA

Middle schoolers need to love people sincerely and honor God in all their relationships.

KEY SCRIPTURES

- *Love for others is the second greatest commandment* (Matt. 22:36-40).
- *Loving others means being devoted to them and putting them before ourselves* (Rom. 12:10).
- *Our closest relationships need to be with people of same-hearted devotion to Christ* (2 Cor. 6:14-18).
- *We need godly relationships* (Ecc. 4:9-12).

KEY QUESTIONS YOUR MIDDLE SCHOOLER IS ASKING

- Why are relationships sometimes so difficult?
- Why won't he/she like me?
- Why do my parents not get along?

AT THIS AGE MOST MIDDLE SCHOOLERS WILL …

- Struggle with peer pressure and social skills in friendships and relationships with the opposite sex.
- Ask broad, unanswerable questions about life including complex moral and ethical questions.
- Want to explore spiritual matters and relationships with others.

DEVELOPMENTAL MILESTONES

- Many middle schoolers will begin to view moral issues in shades of gray rather than only in black and white. They tend to be unprepared to cope with the issues and need the guidance of parents and other adults.
- Middle schoolers can be moody, restless, and display inconsistent behavior. They are often self-conscious and sensitive to criticism which may impact their relationships with others.
- This can be a tumultuous time in their relationships with their parents. While they begin middle school still seeing parents as heroes and fully accepting their authority, that can change as they get older. In their eyes, parents can be seen as stifling who they are and denying them the freedom they feel entitled to.

COACHING TIPS

• If you haven't already, now is the time to discuss dating standards with your middle schooler. You may still be a few years away from allowing him to date, but set the standards now, so that he knows them ahead of time.

• Discuss Romans 12:10 with your middle schooler about what it means to honor people. Point out that regardless of whether someone is deserving of our honor, we are commanded to show honor to others in our actions and speech (1 Tim. 4:12). In fact, Paul says we are to literally "outdo one another in showing honor."

• Middle schoolers have a tendency to be self-absorbed. Everything centers around them. Find creative ways to focus their attention on others. Do service projects together as a family and encourage her to be involved in ministry opportunities through your church's student ministry.

• Remember that you are your middle schooler's model for how to relate to others. He is watching how you relate to your spouse, to his siblings, and to people in the neighborhood and at church. He's noticing how you honor and respect others, especially those who are different than you. Be sure to present a Christlike example.

CONVERSATION STARTERS

• **WHAT DOES IT MEAN TO HONOR SOMEONE?** Honoring someone may be foreign to your middle schooler. This question may give you the opportunity to explain and define the word. And point out how they can better honor those around them.

• **ARE THERE PEOPLE YOU DON'T GET ALONG WITH?** This may give you insight into conflict your middle schooler is facing and provide you the opportunity to help her work through it from a biblical perspective.

• **WHAT DO YOU THINK ABOUT MARRIAGE?** Your middle schooler won't feel pressured by this question, so you can have some fun with it. Talk about characteristics your middle schooler would want in a spouse.

SAY OR PRAY

• Pray that your middle schooler would show grace, respect, and honor in all his relationships.

• Pray specifically for each of your middle schooler's friends. Pray for their salvation, their spiritual growth, and that they would be godly influences in your middle schooler's life.

• Encourage your middle schooler to let you know when she is concerned for a friend and how you can pray for him/her.

BIG IDEA

High schoolers need to love people sincerely and honor God in all their relationships.

KEY SCRIPTURES

- *Love for others is the second greatest commandment* (Matt. 22:36-40).
- *Loving others means being devoted to them and putting them before ourselves* (Rom. 12:10).
- *Our closest relationships need to be with people of same-hearted devotion to Christ* (2 Cor. 6:14-18).
- *We need godly relationships* (Ecc. 4:9-12).

KEY QUESTIONS YOUR HIGH SCHOOLER IS ASKING

- When can I date?
- Why do my parents not get along?
- Why did my boyfriend/girlfriend break up with me?
- Why am I so lonely?

AT THIS AGE MOST HIGH SCHOOLERS WILL ...

- Not be totally confident, but they are more aware of who they are.
- Greatly value the relationships they have with their friends.
- Continue to look to their parents as relationship models.

DEVELOPMENTAL MILESTONES

- High schoolers will move from impulsive and mercurial friendships with peers that are activity-based to stable friendships based on ideas and shared values.
- Their peer friendships become more intimate and supportive. The older high schoolers get, the less drama accompanies their friendships.
- At this age, high schoolers are looking for a more adult-type relationship with their parents. Though this desire can produce conflict over authority and boundaries, it does set the stage for the eventual friendship relationship between parent and child.
- High schoolers are more aware of possible tension and conflict in the home between parents or between parents and other siblings.

COACHING TIPS

- Make sure dating standards are known, discussed, and upheld with your high schooler. Hopefully, you have already had conversations about how and when dating will take place. If not, you're not too far down the road to back up and set up standards that reflect godly wisdom.
- Be aware that your relationship with your spouse is not going unnoticed by your high schooler. He is learning from you what marriage is about and how to treat a spouse.
- Be prepared to walk through romantic and friendship breakups with your high schooler. Be careful not to make light of these relationship difficulties, remembering a broken heart at any age is painful. At the same time, keep pointing her toward the future during these seasons.
- Work to keep your high schooler connected to his grandparents or grandparent-type people in your church. This relationship will be beneficial and rewarding for both parties. Your high schooler can glean godly wisdom and may feel more freedom to talk with his grandparents about a difficult issue than he does with you.

CONVERSATION STARTERS

- **WHAT WOULD BE THE PERFECT DATE?** Have fun with this question, perhaps even sharing some funny experiences from your dating history. However, use this conversation to discuss and reinforce godly standards you have established for dating relationships.
- **DO YOU EVER FEEL LONELY?** This may be a difficult question to ask and answer, but it's one that needs to be discussed. While your high schooler may have many social media friends and followers, she may still deal with loneliness.
- **IS THERE ANYTHING YOU WANT TO ASK ABOUT THE RELATIONSHIP BETWEEN YOUR MOM (DAD) AND I?** Dare you be this vulnerable? Remember that just because you give this freedom doesn't mean you have to answer every question. There should be things about your relationship that are kept private. Also, remember you don't have to reveal every detail about a subject. However, this question could lead to some tender and teachable moments, even if the relationship with your spouse is broken.

SAY OR PRAY

- Pray that your high schooler will be surrounded by godly people.
- Pray for your high schooler to make wise choices in dating and friendship relationships.
- Pray that you would be a good model for godly relationships.

BIG IDEA

Young adults need to love people sincerely and honor God in all their relationships.

KEY SCRIPTURES

- *Love for others is the second greatest commandment* (Matt. 22:36-40).
- *Loving others means being devoted to them and putting them before ourselves* (Rom. 12:10).
- *Our closest relationships need to be with people of same-hearted devotion to Christ* (2 Cor. 6:14-18).
- *We need godly relationships* (Ecc. 4:9-12).

KEY QUESTIONS YOUR YOUNG ADULT IS ASKING

- Who should I marry?
- How should I think about dating?
- Why am I still single?
- Why do I struggle with loneliness?

AT THIS AGE MOST YOUNG ADULTS WILL ...

- Be greatly affected by the relationship modeled for them by their parents.
- Value committed relationships.
- Desire to make their own decisions about relationships.
- Tend to think they have reached maturity and will want others to treat them as if they are fully grown.

DEVELOPMENTAL MILESTONES

- Young adults are beginning to look to the future and make long-term goals, including thoughts about marriage and family.
- They continue to want advice and input from the adults in their lives, but they are looking for this help more in the form of guidance rather than instruction.
- Community is very important to young adults. Many of them have left the comfortable communities of family, church, and teenage friends and are looking for new places to fit in and connect.
- Young adults are wanting to engage in more adult social settings. They are looking to move away from teen activities.

COACHING TIPS

- Be a good listener. Remember you have moved from insisting to suggesting. Be a sounding board as they process new relationships and new social settings.
- Be transparent and honest as you give advice on relationships. Talk about your successes and failures in friendships and dating relationships. Make sure they know you and your spouse's courtship story—the positives and the negatives. In all of these situations, focus on lessons learned rather than the details.
- Be prepared to help pick up pieces from broken relationships. Loving someone always runs the risk of being hurt. And this will happen to your young adult, perhaps in both friendships and romantic relationships. Resist the urge to try to fix situations. Be a good listener and offer godly counsel as she processes her broken heart.
- Be careful not to press or joke about single young adults getting married. Continue to affirm who he is in Christ and stress the need for him to follow God's will, whether single or married. Also be careful not to promise things you can't fulfill, like "I know there's someone out there for you."

CONVERSATION STARTERS

- **WHAT ARE YOU LOOKING FOR IN A HUSBAND/WIFE?** Encourage your young adult to create a thoughtful and prayerful list and to keep high standards, even if prospects of this high caliber seem to be slim or non-existent.
- **WHO'S THE HAPPIEST COUPLE YOU KNOW? WHAT DO YOU THINK ARE THE KEYS TO THEIR SUCCESS?** Use this question to talk about what makes a strong marriage. Perhaps you might even encourage your young adult to talk with the couple she named to get their advice on love and marriage.
- **WHAT ARE SOME THINGS A SINGLE PERSON MIGHT BE ABLE TO ACCOMPLISH THAT A MARRIED PERSON COULD NOT DO?** Help your young adult know that being single is not a curse and single people are not second-class citizens. Point out that while single, his opportunities to make an impact for Christ could be expanded and more varied.

SAY OR PRAY

- Pray that your young adult makes close friends with godly people who share a love for Christ and passion for His work.
- But also pray that your young adult builds relationships with those who don't know Christ, and that he would be bold in sharing his faith.
- Pray that whether your young adult gets married or not, she will always find her identity in Christ.

SESSION 6
TECHNOLOGY
NAVIGATING OUR HIGH-TECH WORLD

Use the space below to record notes, quotes, thoughts, and questions from the video panel discussion.

_____

_____

_____

_____

_____

_____

_____

_____

_____

_____

_____

_____

_____

_____

_____

_____

_____

_____

_____

_____

_____

_____

_____

_____

_____

_____

_____

_____

_____

GROUP GUIDE

Use the following questions and prompts to continue the conversation about the issues discussed by the video panel.

What are some benefits we gain from technology? What are some negative effects?

What technology boundaries, if any, do you currently have in your home?

What kind of technology behavior are you modeling for your child? Does your child know that screens don't dominate your life? Explain.

Do you feel the pressure to keep up with technology? If so, are you? Is it really necessary? Why or why not?

What are you doing to create experiences for your child that aren't connected to a screen? Why is this so important?

How does technology steal reflection time from your child? How does it steal innocence? How does it steal connection?

If you have an older child, how do you see social media benefitting him or her? How is it taking a toll on your child?

What would you say currently has the most influence in shaping the character and identity of your child, Scripture or technology? What can you do to position Scripture as the main influence?

How comfortable is your child in saying "I can't" to things their friends and peers seem to be permitted to do? How comfortable are you with this? Explain.

Is the theme "confession is better than concealment" the current atmosphere in your home? If not, how do you foster that attitude?

Would you say technology is a tool in your family, or has it become the boss of your family?

What steps do you need to take to make technology a positive factor in your family and a tool to use to advance God's kingdom?

TAKEAWAYS:

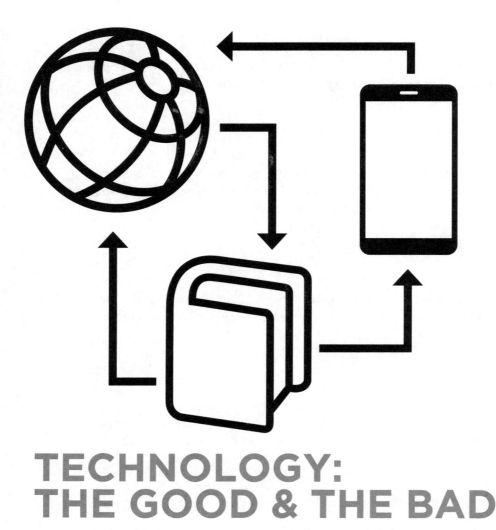

TECHNOLOGY: THE GOOD & THE BAD

I want you to be wise about what is good, and yet innocent about what is evil.
ROMANS 16:19b

TECHNOLOGY OVERLOAD

Our children are engrossed in technology. Unlike many of us, there was never a time when our kids didn't have the Internet or access to personal computers. Most children begin using technology around age two, usually through smartphones or tablets. As they grow up, their engagement with digital media grows with them. From games and shows, to texting, shopping, and social media, there are an unlimited number of ways that technology has become integrated with modern life. And sadly, both statistics and experience tell us that the results are often negative. As Christian parents, it's time we admit that too much technology is dangerous.

In the scope of a lifetime, you have a few short years with your children in your home. Don't give those precious moments away.

Is your family guilty? Do you hand your kids a phone or a tablet in the afternoon and let them check out? Work is exhausting. You have a thousand things to check off your list between leaving the office and putting your head down on your pillow at night. But one thing you absolutely cannot neglect is quality time with your kids. Christ-centered parenting is intentional parenting. In the scope of a lifetime, you have a few short years with your children in your home. Don't give those precious moments away. Don't let the pale light of a screen raise your children for you.

A GREAT TOOL, BUT A DANGEROUS MASTER

Technology isn't going away. But that's not necessarily a bad thing. As we discuss this issue, let's be clear that technology in and of itself is not evil. We can all appreciate the gifts of modern technology—microwaves, cars, and yes, even smartphones. The danger for our kids is not the technology itself but when and how they use it.

The digital revolution has changed our lives. Unfortunately, it has also opened the door to certain kinds of temptations that were previously unimaginable. This is the reality for our children's generation. They will contend every day with temptations that many of us have never known. And this leads us to a simple point: Christian parents must not allow their children to use computers, smartphones, or tablets that have unrestricted Internet access.

Hear this as a plea. We know what happens when sexually-forming minds are exposed to pornography. We know the kind of pull to temptation, especially among young males, that comes with the promise of sexual "fulfillment," even more so with the illusion of anonymity. And we know that predators use the Internet to troll for naïve children to exploit.

So how could we possibly put our children in a situation of that sort of peril?

We ought to know better than this. And we don't mean that Christians ought to know better. It's worse than that. Human beings ought to know better. It doesn't take the indwelling Holy Spirit to know that turning a middle schooler or teenager loose with unrestricted Internet access is insane.

Jesus described the Fatherhood of God by noting that no one, not even an evil person, would give his son a serpent when he asked for a fish (Matt. 7:10). Why not? It's because natural affection propels a father to seek to protect his child from something harmful.

But sadly, we live in a culture, even in our Christian circles, that is willing to give a child a serpent, as long as he really wants it. After all, all his friends have access to venomous reptiles and we don't want him to feel different. Besides, we "trust" him.

Brothers and sisters and friends, this is madness.

Don't miss our point—we think the digital revolution is largely a good thing. Children should be reared to see technology as a tool to be used for kingdom priorities. But there's far too much at stake to turn a developing psyche loose, with no boundaries, on a technology that could psychically and spiritually cripple him or her (and a future family, too) for a lifetime. Technology is good. Turning our children over to the cyber-wilderness is not.[1]

We don't have to rid our lives of technology and boycott the Internet. Instead, as we "take every thought captive to obey Christ" (2 Cor. 10:5), we redeem our technology use for good. If we truly believe that God is concerned with every aspect of our lives, then we will learn to use technology for His glory.

CRUCIAL QUESTIONS

Here are questions to ask your kids (and yourself) regarding technology use:

• Are you being true to who you are as an image-bearer of God? Do you feel any shame about something you posted online or about the way you are using an app or video game?

• Is this honoring your relationships with other people? Are you saying things that are demeaning, derogatory, or manipulative? Are you giving respect to the people you encounter online who are made in the image of God?

• Does your activity online and on mobile apps bring glory to God?[2]

What picture are your children presenting to the world? Is it an accurate representation of who they are? Is it an honest picture of your family? Are they pointing others to

Christ with their witness on social media or putting a stumbling block in someone's path?

OTHER AREAS TO CONSIDER

Thinking through our children's use of technology includes more than surfing the Internet and watching too much TV. Playing video games is an extremely popular activity. While children are usually drawn to video games for entertainment, there are a number of reasons to monitor the use of video games in your home.

Here are a few things to consider. Video games can be highly addictive. Make sure your child's gaming doesn't become an idol or an obsession. Kids sometimes turn to video games to escape from pressures or problems in their life—a child will seek success in a digital world to mask perceived failures or struggles in the real world. Some games simply have inappropriate content. It is always good for you to know what your child is being exposed to. And finally, consider the amount of time your child spends playing these games. Too much attention to gaming can easily cause your child to neglect things like family, school, and Christ.

Another concern that is becoming more and more popular among teens and young adults is known as sexting (sending sexual images of oneself through technology). This is another challenge of the digital age, and it is one that may affect your kids before they are mature enough to understand it. Some kids admit that they sent these images or videos because of pressure from another person, but often this happens simply because the child is too young or immature to grasp the consequences of his or her actions.[3]

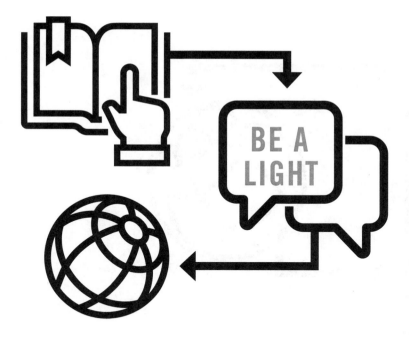

As parents, we must be prepared to respond. On a practical level, reiterate the damage this can do to their reputation and remind them that sending and receiving explicit pictures of a person under the age of 18 is illegal. Help them see beyond today and look ahead to their future spouse and children.[4] But don't forget to take them back to the basics of the purpose of their sexuality. Sexual intimacy is designed for marriage. It is holy and special. Sexting is a cheap imitation of God's design, and it bears permanent consequences.[5]

REDEEMING THE GIFT

Help your child understand both the positives and negatives of technology. In Genesis 1, we see God's work in the garden at creation and He pronounced it "good." But we know the next chapter in the story. Man sinned and the good things God gave him became burdensome. His work was made difficult. The blessing of bearing children became painful.

The gifts are tainted. Technology is a good gift, but it can easily be used for sinful ends. Let's help our kids redeem this gift and live "as shrewd as serpents and as innocent as doves" (Matt. 10:16) in the online world.

QUESTIONS FOR REFLECTION

1. Do you think this article comes down too hard on technology? Why or why not?

2. How has technology changed the dynamics of your family life over the last few years, both positively and negatively?

3. What changes do you personally need to make in the area of technology use?

4. What one thing stood out to you from this article?

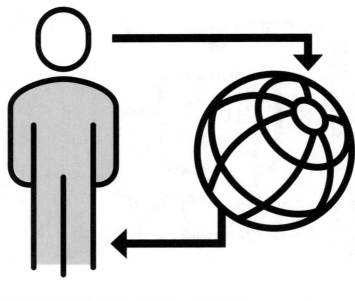

SETTING UP BOUNDARIES

Set your minds on things above,
not on earthly things.
COLOSSIANS 3:2

Internet technology is here to stay. In so many ways, the Internet and digital media have become integrated into our everyday lives. But as we've seen, this technology presents many unique challenges for Christian parents and their children. As parents, we need to think carefully about the best ways to equip our children to use this technology responsibly, but we must also prayerfully consider how we will act to protect our kids from the dangers and pitfalls of technology. All of this will require serious effort.

Many parents falsely assume that setting up simple boundaries and parameters for online activity is an adequate solution.

Of course boundaries are a necessary and helpful step, but the real issue lies deeper. Our real concern as parents is to make sure that—in addition to monitoring the use of technology in our home—we are constantly monitoring the hearts of our children. This is necessary because, ultimately, the technology isn't the problem. Instead, it is our use of things like smartphones and computers that reveals the sinful desires in our hearts.

If we are to raise our children to use technology in a responsible way, then this will certainly include setting up appropriate boundaries; it will also require us to teach our children how to root out idols (1 John 5:18-21). This is about more than protecting them from evil; it is about teaching them to pursue what is good (Rom. 12:9).

One of the best ways to keep your kids from living behind a screen is to make sure your family is actively enjoying life together.

SHOULD MY KID HAVE A SMARTPHONE?

Pornography is the greatest danger to children with unrestricted Internet access. And make no mistake, the porn industry is targeting your child. Porn is more trafficked on the Internet than Netflix, Amazon, and Twitter combined.[6] The industry is constantly in search of new consumers, and it has no issue exploiting young children. For this reason, allowing your child unrestricted access to the Internet is a recipe for disaster (especially via a smartphone with a private browsing history).

Our children are incredibly vulnerable. Making a decision about smartphones isn't the same as deciding whether or not to allow your child to watch television. In fact, the danger presented by television pales in comparison to the immense danger of unfettered Internet access. Pornography is highly addictive, very dangerous, and widely available online for free. Pornography preys on our God-given sexual desires, permanently embeds explicit images into our brains, and conditions us with unhealthy sexual expectations. And beyond the danger of pornography itself, secret ("private") use of the Internet also exposes our children to the danger of online predators or the pressures of an adolescent culture that encourages things like sexting.

Because the danger is so great, we do not recommend that you allow young children to own a smartphone that has easy access to the Internet, even if you are committed to using programs that block inappropriate sites. It is simply too easy for those programs to be circumvented, and it isn't worth potentially exposing your child to these risks in the name of digital freedom.

As your children get older and they demonstrate increased levels of maturity and responsibility, you can gradually begin giving them more and more freedom. At some point, you might consider allowing them to own a smartphone for the first time. In this case, make every effort to prepare them to use it responsibly. Install accountability software on the phone and have the accountability reports sent to you. Understand that being cautious with technology isn't about trying to shelter our kids—it is about protecting them from unnecessary danger.[7]

A DIFFERENT APPROACH

Too often we assume that taking a different approach to things like technology will cause our kids to miss out on fun things other kids are doing. In this case, the opposite is true. We believe that taking a holistic approach to raising our children actually offers them a better and more enjoyable childhood. By monitoring the amount of time our kids spend behind a screen, we free them up to enjoy and pursue things that are even better for them.

One of the best ways to keep your kids from living behind a screen is to make sure your family is actively enjoying life together. Get outside and enjoy nature. Teach your kids to ride bikes, play catch, and jump in the leaves. Go camping. Make a habit of taking walks together as a family. Take your kids to the neighborhood playground. Whatever your family likes to do, go do it together and focus on engaging with one another. There are countless benefits to this approach—improved social skills (like taking turns), increased attention span, and reduced stress just to name a few.[8]

Another way to combat an unhealthy digital dependence is to encourage more time with friends. We have previously discussed the tremendous benefits of community. Making time for your younger kids to play with other children and teaching your older children to build relationships without the distraction of handheld technology is a great way for them to learn to value people as people. Human interaction is being diminished in our digital age, but knowing and enjoying other people is not only an important life skill—it is part of the reason that God made us.

It is also critical for us to model this as parents. Our children learn their habits from us. Make sure you are engaged in conversations at the dinner table and not just checking your phone. Create time in your family's rhythms to enjoy and spend time with one another. Invite others into your home and model the kind of hospitality and conversation you want your kids to emulate. And as much as possible, be sure that the parents also abide by the "house rules" for using technology. Your faithfulness and consistency shows your kids what really matters.

The goal of Christ-centered parenting is always to instruct our children in the ways of the Lord while they are in our homes so that when they are on their own, they will know how to live. Even though we have encouraged parents to monitor the ways technology is used in the home, we also believe that parents must train their kids to use technology responsibly. Train your child to use technology well by using it well yourself. Don't allow it to dominate your life or draw you into sin. At the same time, do not teach your kids to live in fear of it either. Technology is a gift that can enhance their lives. Take the lead in teaching them how to use it.

A PRACTICAL GUIDE TO SETTING BOUNDARIES

Technology exposes our idolatry. Combating the misuse or overuse of technology is important, but parents must always remember that a child's behavior is nothing more than a reflection of his or her heart. And just like yours, those hearts are full of idols. But as you work toward these deeper issues, setting up appropriate boundaries can be very helpful. Here are some helpful ways to do just that:

ALLOW YOUR CHILD TO DEMONSTRATE RESPONSIBILITY IN LESS CONSEQUENTIAL WAYS BEFORE GIVING THEM TOO MUCH FREEDOM. For younger children, this could be as simple as setting a time limit on the use of a tablet or game console and allowing them to enforce the limit themselves. For older kids, it might be permission to establish social media accounts that you have the ability to monitor.

MAKE SURE THE LINES OF COMMUNICATION ARE OPEN. Create an environment that encourages your kids

As much as possible, be sure that the parents also abide by the "house rules" for using technology. Your faithfulness and consistency shows your kids what really matters.

to come to you and to be honest with you about issues they face. If you know they have misused technology or been exposed to inappropriate content, give them the opportunity to speak about it honestly. Show them grace and help them overcome the temptation to lie or be deceitful.

SET MUTUALLY AGREED UPON LIMITS. As you determine these boundaries, allow your child to have input, and take those feelings into consideration. Explain the purpose of the limits. Help them see the positives in limiting screen time, and let them know you're on their side.

FOR YOUNGER KIDS, TAKE A HANDS-ON APPROACH. Set definitive time limits for technology use and stick to them. Know what they are watching and playing, and have the necessary filters in place. Everything should go through your eyes first.

FOR OLDER KIDS, TAKE FULL ADVANTAGE OF TECHNOLOGY-MONITORING SOFTWARE. You don't have time to police every activity. Set up software that will allow you to see who they are talking to online, and let them know that you will have access to who they call and text on all devices. Emphasize that you are on their side and these measures are in place for their protection, not their punishment.

FINALLY, DON'T PUT TOO MUCH FAITH IN YOUR BOUNDARIES. It's easy to ride on cruise control thinking, "We have

filters, so we're good." But the truth is, your kids, who are much more technologically savvy than you are, can find ways around filters and parental controls. More importantly, your children are sinners. Sin bleeds into every area of our lives and affects everything we do. If your child has access to technology, sin will lead to transgression and boundaries will be crossed.

This is a difficult burden. Our advice is to pray hard. Give grace as much as possible. Always let your kids know that they can come to you when they make mistakes. And always point them back to Jesus.

QUESTIONS FOR REFLECTION

1. What boundaries do you currently have in place for yourself and your family when it comes to technology use?

2. How are you actively helping your child to use technology wisely?

3. How does your family enjoy life together away from screens?

4. What further steps will you take now to protect the minds and hearts of your family?

5. What one thing stood out to you from this article?

SOCIAL MEDIA

Do not be conformed to this age, but be transformed by the renewing of your mind, so that you may discern what is the good, pleasing, and perfect will of God.
ROMANS 12:2

Social media is a recent phenomenon that has introduced new challenges to both children and parents. Social networks exist to connect people with other people. And in many ways, this technology can serve to enhance our lives. But as many parents have discovered, the world of social media can easily prove distracting, or worse, become a catalyst for sinful behavior. With technology in constant flux and a lack of biblical instruction on the subject, it is easy to understand why so many parents are unsure about the best way to guide their kids through the complexities of social networking.

No one has all the answers to these questions. For this reason, we simply offer some basic guidelines and principles that are grounded in biblical wisdom.

THE GREENER GRASS ON THE OTHER SIDE

If you've spent any amount of time on social media, you may have an idea of the possible perils in the online friendship world. Some assume that social media is only guilty of being a major timewaster, but the actual dangers run much deeper.

Author Vicki Courtney relates the story of a mother whose 12-year-old daughter had begun cutting. Courtney writes:

The discovery came as a complete shock to the mother who said it was out of character for her daughter to engage in such a risky behavior. She was a straight-A student and involved in extracurricular activities. In addition to having two loving and engaged parents in the home, she also had many close friends and was involved in her church youth group.

The mother went on to share that after several counseling sessions, the root of the problem had been discovered. They had recently allowed their daughter to use a popular social media app with some time limitations and protective boundaries in place. She was required to keep her account private and give her mother her login information so her mother could monitor her activity from time to time. Even so, the mother didn't notice any unusual activity that might have triggered her daughter's cutting. And that was the problem. There were no comments that implied bullying.

> *As parents, we must teach our kids to love and find joy in the real life God has given them, not the fake life that is carefully presented to digital followers.*

Nor was there any contact from a stranger making inappropriate requests. Her daughter confessed to the counselor that she began cutting herself because she felt worthless when she compared herself to everyone else's highlight reel. The triggers weren't obvious, but at the same time, they were out in the open for all to see.

Her daughter struggled to understand why some of her friends' pictures got more likes than her pictures. Or why some of the girls she thought were her friends didn't mutually follow her back. She was stressed over pictures of girls who she perceived to be prettier and more fashionable and had the comments and likes from the popular boys to prove it, or the pictures of some of her friends hanging out together, without her. She began to obsess over perfectly timed posts with witty status updates that might garner her more likes and followers, but it never seemed to be enough. The more time she spent on the app, the more worthless she felt.[9]

Social media fuels comparison and envy, especially for young people. It creates the illusion that there is always someone with a better life—a cuter boyfriend, better grades, prettier hair, a fancier car, or a better family. Even well-adjusted kids from loving, engaged families can fall victim to the empty promises on the other side of the screen.

The perfectly-timed and -filtered photos we post to social media provide a running stream of Hollywood highlight reels, which create a mirage of constant happiness. But most often, it is only a mirage. As parents, we must teach our kids to love and find joy in the real life God has given them, not the fake life that is carefully presented to digital followers.

POTENTIAL PITFALLS

Social media can easily distort reality or isolate the user. One way that you can prepare your kids to use social media well is to help them identify some of the potential pitfalls inherent to the world of online friendship.

Consider the following examples:

SOCIAL MEDIA IS NOT ALWAYS REALITY. These online networks allow people to present themselves in an ideal way—users highlight their best qualities and carefully omit any flaws. Obviously, there is more going on behind the scenes.

SOCIAL MEDIA FOSTERS LONELINESS. The online world gives the appearance of relationships, but many of those relationships don't transfer into real life. The more time they spend online, they more they prefer fake relationships to real ones.

SOCIAL MEDIA LEADS TO A LACK OF REAL, GENUINE CONNECTION WITH FLESH AND BLOOD PEOPLE. While social media gives us the ability to stay connected to many different groups of people, it can put up a wall between us and those we see every day. Real relationships are hard. The more time your kids spend on social media, the more they lose the hands-on skills needed to be successful in their most important relationships.

SOCIAL MEDIA MISDIRECTS IDENTITY. One of the tragedies of frequent use of social media is the fact that it can quickly become a metric for evaluating one's worth. This is especially common among young people. More than simply comparing themselves to the friends and celebrities they follow online, social media users can become obsessed with the validation that comes from gaining likes and followers.

Make sure you and your child are aware of these pitfalls and have a plan to avoid them.

THE NEED FOR HUMAN CONNECTION

Although in theory our pre-teens and teenagers may be constantly connected to other people through social networks like Facebook, Instagram, and Twitter, they are still in desperate need of real, human interaction. Author and girls' ministry leader Erin Davis writes:

The teenagers in your world need a hug. They need eye contact. They need someone to sit across from them in an actual coffee shop and carry on a conversation without emojis. Since Titus 2 calls all of us to invest in the next generation, this is important news. We don't have to be cool. (Thank goodness!) We don't have to develop slick programs. We don't have to write or speak in teenager jargon. As we seek to disciple young people, the plan is simple: give them what they crave, human connection, and then point them to Jesus. You can do that![10]

As image-bearers of the Triune God, we are designed to live in relationship with one another. One of the best things you could do for your son or daughter today is to put away all the devices (theirs and yours) and just talk. No agenda. No script. Just conversation.

Sit down with your family and read Acts 2 where we see the kind of community experienced in the early days of the church.

They devoted themselves to the apostles' teaching, to the fellowship, to the breaking of bread, and to prayer.
ACTS 2:42

The church is described as a community that gathers together to worship, to pray, and to be encouraged by one another. Let the local church be the place where your children find community. They need to be there when God's people are gathered, to know and bear the burdens of their peers.

Carry one another's burdens; in this way you will fulfill the law of Christ.
GALATIANS 6:2

Study the Word together, and learn to pray for one another.

A HUMAN DIGNITY ISSUE

Our identity as God's image-bearers is absolutely crucial to every area of Christ-centered parenting. We are living, breathing representations of the Almighty God. Does this truth have an impact on what your kids post on social media? Is their identity rooted in who they are online or who they are in Christ? Do they have a sense of identity that isn't based on someone else's social media presence? Do they treat people with dignity when they interact with them online?

Social media gives everyone the opportunity to be somebody, pushing our kids into a culture obsessed with fame. Anyone with a smartphone and an ounce of wit can be a celebrity online. Your kids are so much more than who they are on social media. This is only a small part of their identities. They are not defined by how many followers they have or how many people like their status. They are image-bearers of the living God.

A HEALTHY BALANCE

It will take great care and intentionality to make sure that social media plays an appropriate role in your child's life. One of the most important ways to do this is to balance social media use with other priorities. Start by promoting a sense of authentic, biblical community in your home. Share meals at the dinner table and discuss the issues weighing on your son or daughter's heart. Set aside family times that are private. Don't post every activity online. Make these times special for your kids.

If your child is using social media, continue to encourage him or her to spend time with friends that you trust. Invite those friends to your table to promote real, significant relationships in your child's life.

Keep a healthy perspective on social media. If it is causing anxiety in your children's life, then take a break. If it is promoting a negative view of self, delete it. Don't allow social media to become an idol. Instead, keep their eyes set on the most important friend they have—the One who knows them inside and out and will never leave them or forsake them (Heb. 13:5).

QUESTIONS FOR REFLECTION

1. Assess how social media is being used by members of your family. Is it healthy? Do you have a good understanding of the different platforms being used? Explain.

2. How are you doing at making face-to-face time with your child a priority? What changes can you make to increase this time?

3. How are you promoting authentic biblical community in your home?

4. What one thing stood out to you from this article?

BIG IDEA

Teach and model healthy technology habits that preschoolers can develop as they grow.

KEY SCRIPTURES

- *God does not want us to waste our time* (Eph. 5:15-16).
- *God is the most important* (Matt. 6:33).
- *God wants us to trust in Him* (Ps. 37:5).
- *God want us to make good decisions* (1 Cor. 6:12).
- *God wants us to do everything for Him* (1 Cor. 10:31).

KEY QUESTIONS YOUR PRESCHOOLER IS ASKING

- Why can't I play my game on the tablet whenever I want?
- Why can't I watch that movie?
- Why can't I do what my older brother or sister does?

AT THIS AGE MOST PRESCHOOLERS WILL …

- Understand the technology of smartphones and tablets.
- Refine fine motor skills via touch screens.
- Develop longer attention spans.

DEVELOPMENTAL MILESTONES

- Preschoolers' minds are incredibly impressionable, so nearly everything they see or experience makes an impact on their development. For this reason, it is important that you strictly limit and control their intake of media or technology.
- Children at this age often have lots of energy and likely have trouble sitting still. Rather than using a tablet or television to occupy your child, provide alternatives, like playing a board game, reading, coloring, or playing outside. Hands-on creative play is essential for healthy development. Too much screen time for children has also been found to have a negative effect on brain development.
- At this age children are developing hand-eye coordination and fine motor skills. Apps and games that encourage these skills will benefit your child when she begins to write, play sports, or learn an instrument. Research educational apps that will further your child's set of skills or interests.

COACHING TIPS

- Although it can be tempting to use technology as a quick babysitter, interactive media is most beneficial when collaborative. Interactive technology engages your child more than television, but making the game interpersonal will employ even more areas of the brain. Talk through the game with your child, discussing his problem-solving strategies and approaches. Be sure to use apps appropriate for your child's age range and milestones, and test them before your child plays them.
- As always, setting a good example is the most effective teaching tool. Exhibit healthy habits, like not using your phone during meals or turning the TV off when it isn't being used. Emphasize spending time together as a family instead of being too glued to technology. The earlier in life that healthy habits are established, the better. Be sure your child does not become dependent upon technology as a means for curing boredom, problem solving, or entertainment in general.
- Set clear time limits and boundaries for your child's technology use. For preschoolers, 20 to 30 minutes of screen time twice a day is the recommended maximum. Treat screen time and TV as a special privilege rather than something they expect or feel entitled to have. This way your child understands priorities and learns not to depend on technology.

CONVERSATION STARTERS

- **WHAT DO YOU THINK WILL HAPPEN NEXT?** Make apps and games more interactive by playing them *with* your child. Prompt your child to answer questions about the game, pausing to ask what he thinks will happen next or why he made a certain decision.
- **HOW CAN THIS HELP IN REAL LIFE?** Draw comparisons between enjoyment from technology and real-life situations. Discuss what real-life things bring your child joy, and emphasize how these things can help your child grow and learn. Even while using technology, consider realistic applications your child could use with the skills she is using in technology.
- **WHAT CAN WE DO NOW THAT THE ELECTRONICS ARE OFF? HOW CAN WE USE OUR IMAGINATIONS TO PLAY?** Give your preschooler blank paper and crayons or makers, modeling clay, or LEGO® bricks—anything that you can use to create. Your imagination is the limit!

SAY OR PRAY

- We should use our time to honor God.
- Everything we do should honor God.
- Good decisions are ones that follow God's way.
- Honoring God is the most important thing in our lives.

BIG IDEA

Teach and model healthy technology habits that children can develop further as they grow.

KEY SCRIPTURES

- *God does not want us to waste our time* (Eph. 5:15-16).
- *God is the most important* (Matt. 6:33).
- *God wants us to trust in Him* (Ps. 37:5).
- *God want us to make good decisions* (1 Cor. 6:12).
- *God wants us to do everything for Him* (1 Cor. 10:31).

KEY QUESTIONS YOUR ELEMENTARY-AGED CHILD IS ASKING

- Why can't I have more screen time?
- All my friends are playing that video game. Why can't I?
- Why do you limit what I can see on the Internet?

AT THIS AGE MOST ELEMENTARY CHILDREN WILL …

- Become increasingly more independent.
- Have the tendency to spend prolonged amounts of time absorbed in activities that interest them.
- Rapidly develop physical, cognitive, and social skills.

DEVELOPMENTAL MILESTONES

- Younger elementary age children need security and structure. Working together to set technology boundaries will help provide a sense of both. Involving him in your decisions also encourages his developing sense of responsibility. If your child will have access to a computer or tablet at home, insist the device be kept in a family area, and set parental controls to block inappropriate Internet access.
- Children at this age have good hand-eye coordination. Many video games and apps can stimulate that coordination, although too much time involved in these activities can limit development in other areas. Check out the games and apps your child is using to make sure they are high quality, age appropriate activities.
- Peer pressure becomes more challenging for kids at this age, as they struggle to belong and fit in. Avoid "because I said so" responses as your child seeks answers to the boundaries you set for her. Use biblical principles as you explain your decisions to limit her access to and use of technology.

COACHING TIPS

- Remember that kids may understand technology better than you do, so they may be able to bypass controls you set up. Enlist the help of tech-savvy people to enable restrictions to safeguard your child.
- Establish a clear time limit on your child's use of technology, like one or two hours a day. Involve your child in negotiating technology time limits during a family meeting. Develop a contract to outline details. Consider allowing your child to earn extra technology time by doing something constructive, helpful, active, or creative. Help your child understand that screen time is a privilege, not something they are entitled to have.
- Set an example for your child by limiting your own use of technology. Encourage your family to observe "no technology times" in your home, like supper time. Also encourage spending family time together doing activities like hiking, working puzzles, or playing board games.

CONVERSATION STARTERS

- **WHAT DO YOU WANT TO DO TODAY?** As you and your child make plans for the upcoming day, invite her to think through activities she'd like to do. Help her to evaluate the activities and make good decisions based on quality use of her time.
- **WHAT DO YOU THINK MY JOB AS A PARENT IS?** Often kids will question why parents make the decisions they do regarding their child's activities. Help your child understand your God-given responsibility to care for and protect him. Explain that the boundaries you set are your best attempt to be the parent God wants you to be.
- **WHAT ARE YOU WATCHING (LOOKING AT, READING, PLAYING, ETC.)?** As you notice your child engaged in playing a game or looking at something on a screen, invite her to tell you about it. Look at the material yourself. Periodically checking and evaluating what your child is exposed to is a parent's right and responsibility. If the material is inappropriate, help your child understand why and take steps to avoid future access to that information.

SAY OR PRAY

- Everything we do should honor God, including the way we use our time.
- Good decisions are ones that follow God's teachings.
- We can trust that God's ways are the best ways.

BIG IDEA

Develop healthy technology habits in your child as she grows.

KEY SCRIPTURES

- *God does not want us to waste our time* (Eph. 5:15-17).
- *God wants us to form our identities in Christ* (Rom. 15:5-7; Phil. 2:1-5).
- *God gives us wisdom and understanding* (Prov. 2:6).
- *We are to not be subject to technology, but use it for God's purpose* (Gen. 1:28).
- *God wants us to make good decisions* (Prov. 3:5-6; 1 Cor. 6:12).
- *God is more important than anyone or anything else* (Matt. 6:33).

KEY QUESTIONS YOUR PRETEEN MAY ASK

- Why can't I play that game/watch that movie/visit that website?
- Can I have that?
- Why do people act differently online than they do in real life?

AT THIS AGE MOST PRETEENS WILL …

- Be highly literate in touchscreen interfaces and text communication.
- Be interested in movies, TV, video games, and social media platforms.
- Be coming into and exploring their identities.

DEVELOPMENTAL MILESTONES

- Preteens will gravitate naturally toward things that connote social power, popularity, and/or acceptance. The newest technology quickly grows obsolete. Your preteen will probably want some of the newest products. Be sure to put these trends into context. This will promote a higher understanding of what needs and wants really are and increase her ability to self-limit later.
- Preteens often find themselves idling in front of a screen. This sort of behavior has been proven scientifically to have a negative effect on brain development. Talk to your child's pediatrician about wise choices. Physical health and fitness can play an important part in overall body image and emotional development.
- Even if your preteen is not using social media yet, she may want to before long. Because preteens are rigorously aware of social roles and thirst for approval, friendship, and belonging, they may see social media platforms as a way of furthering or of rounding out their identities. Help direct your preteen toward a healthy and Christlike understanding of herself.

- At this age, preteens will be approaching their athletic prime. Encourage their interests in sports as well as in other extracurricular activities.

COACHING TIPS

- Monitor your preteen's access to the Internet and TV. If your preteen has a phone, establish rules for its use. Place computers in public areas and install software safeguards. Discuss the pros and cons of technology. Explain your reasons for boundaries, lending perspective to your authority, and helping your child understand the restrictions.
- Don't let technology dictate how you and your family do life. Use it wisely in ways that honor God and help accomplish His purpose.
- You determine what you allow your child to watch. Discuss how certain content depicts scenes, themes, or worldviews that dishonor God. Allowing your child to watch questionable content will probably be a case-by-case judgment call, but talking with your preteen helps him develop a healthy way of thinking about these things.
- Set a good example. Exhibit healthy habits yourself. Emphasize spending time together as a family instead of being glued to technology. Be sure your preteen does not become dependent upon technology as a means for curing boredom, problem solving, or entertainment in general.

CONVERSATION STARTERS

- **HAVE YOU FINISHED YOUR HOMEWORK?** Create a healthy balance with technology by making it a reward instead of a right. Make sure your preteen knows that many things take priority over a favorite show, game, or website. Quiet time, Bible study, physical play, sports, reading, and hanging out with friends are more important than screen time.
- **WHAT ARE YOUR FRIENDS INTERESTED IN?** This question will help you take inventory of trends in popular culture that may be influencing your preteen. Oftentimes, these trends are OK, but some could be problematic and require discussing with your child.
- **HOW CAN THIS HELP IN REAL LIFE?** Discuss what real-life things bring joy to your child and emphasize how these things can help your child grow and learn. Consider how your child could use the skills she is mastering with technology to help others and honor God.

SAY OR PRAY

- Everything we do should please God.
- Honoring God is the most important thing in life.
- We can use technology to glorify God.

BIG IDEA

Middle schoolers should use technology in healthy, God-honoring ways.

KEY SCRIPTURES

- *We should be discerning when it comes to our use of technology* (1 Chron. 12:32).
- *We should reflect Christ in what we communicate online* (Prov. 17:27).
- *We should be above reproach with what we allow into our lives* (Ps. 101:1-3).
- *Nothing should be our master except Jesus* (1 Cor. 6:12).

KEY QUESTIONS YOUR MIDDLE SCHOOLER IS ASKING

- When can I get a Facebook (Twitter, Snapchat, Instagram) account?
- Why do I need boundaries when it comes to video games and social media?
- How can I get more likes and comments on my pictures and posts?

AT THIS AGE MOST MIDDLE SCHOOL STUDENTS WILL …

- Feel pressured from their peer group to become more involved on social media.
- Begin to see access to social media as a rite of passage in today's culture.
- See social structures very differently because of social media than generations of the past.
- Live out desires of adventure and fantasy through means of video games and virtual reality.

DEVELOPMENTAL MILESTONES

- In middle school, students often strengthen their problem-solving and thinking skills. They may pay more attention to making decisions, including helping to set their own boundaries with technology and social media. They are able to go through "what if" scenarios and talk through potential challenges with technology.
- Middle school is a time of major social and emotional growth. They are often sensitive to the opinions and reactions of others and may think the whole world is watching them. Their self-image can also take a hit if they are disappointed in the number of likes they receive on social media.
- Middle schoolers are part of the technological generation. They are not intimidated by new technology and are usually more tech-savvy than their parents.

COACHING TIPS

- While setting boundaries may be difficult, by doing so you are demonstrating your love for your child. Set godly standards for technology use in your home that are clear. Limit the amount of access to the Internet that you give your child. You can give your middle schooler opportunity to speak into the boundaries, but keep in mind you are the parent and you are accountable.

- Social media is not all negative, but it can be a destructive force in your middle schooler's life if not kept in perspective and regulated. You might want to limit the social platforms your middle schooler is allowed to be on and maintain watch over those accounts. Remember, if you have provided your middle schooler with a phone, it's not his, it's yours. That gives you the right to know how it's being used.

- Inform your middle schooler that much damage has been done through inappropriate emails and text messages. Help your middle schooler understand the need to be careful about what we say and post. Proverbs 17:27 reminds us that fewer words are better than many, and "one who keeps a cool head is a person of understanding." When it comes to social media, never write something in anger.

- Point out that technology in and of itself is not a negative thing. Discuss how to use this tool to honor God and further the gospel.

CONVERSATION STARTERS

- **HOW ARE YOUR FRIENDS USING SOCIAL MEDIA?** Learn how prevalent social media is among your middle schooler's friends, and identify the latest and most popular platform being used. You can follow up by asking how social media can be used to honor God.

- **WHAT DO YOU THINK ARE SOME DANGERS OF TECHNOLOGY?** Make sure to give your middle schooler time to answer before unloading your list. Remember, this is a conversation, not a lecture. After you discuss the dangers, talk about how to use technology wisely and for good.

- **WHAT ARE YOU LEARNING IN YOUR QUIET TIME?** Instead of a frontal attack on time spent on technology versus time with God, approach the subject in this way. Talk with your middle schooler about what he's studying in his devotional time and how you can help this time be more meaningful to him. It's likely that part of the conversation will move to stewardship of time.

SAY OR PRAY

- Pray that God would give you and your middle schooler the grace and wisdom to use technology in a way that honors Him.

- Pray for protection for your middle schooler's eyes, ears, and heart as she engages in technology and social media. Ask God to make her sensitive to the Holy Spirit's leading and to give her courage to walk away from situations, people, or places where technology is being used in an ungodly way.

BIG IDEA

High schoolers should use technology in healthy, God-honoring ways.

KEY SCRIPTURES

- *We should be discerning when it comes to our use of technology* (1 Chron. 12:32).
- *We should reflect Christ in what we communicate online* (Prov. 17:27).
- *We should be above reproach with what we allow into our lives* (Ps. 101:1-3).
- *Nothing should be our master except Jesus* (1 Cor. 6:12).

KEY QUESTIONS YOUR HIGH SCHOOLER IS ASKING

- How can I gain more friends and followers on social media?
- When can I update my phone?
- What's wrong with sharing personal things on social media?

AT THIS AGE MOST HIGH SCHOOLERS WILL …

- Have a smartphone and be closely attached to it.
- Live in a tech-saturated environment, whether they are at home, at school, on the job, and so forth.
- Live out desires of adventure and fantasy through means of video games and virtual reality.
- Be more tech-savvy than their parents.

DEVELOPMENTAL MILESTONES

- Even though high schoolers are growing in maturity, they still struggle to weigh the consequences of their actions. This can result in social media choices that hurt others and reflect badly on themselves.
- High schoolers have the ability to self-regulate their technology use but may struggle to do so. While they may outwardly balk at boundaries placed around technology, most will inwardly welcome the protection and direction.
- Most high schoolers have never known a time when technology was not part of their lives. So while parents and other adults may struggle to adjust to new and fast-paced technological advances, they take it in stride as part of normal living.

COACHING TIPS

- Be wise about the technology access you give to your high schooler. Lay ground rules for phone and technology use. Provide opportunity for him to speak into these boundaries. Encourage your high schooler to be more discerning about his use of technology and a little less passive in his consumption.
- Be aware and alert to the changing apps and social media that high schoolers are using. You don't need to be proficient on every app or be on every social media platform, but keep a good source for this information close, probably someone just a bit older than your high schooler.
- Remind your high schooler that her value and significance is not found in how many friends and followers she has on social media. Keep pointing her to who she is in Christ as the center point in life.
- Monitor your own use of technology. Remember you are setting the example in front of your high schooler about healthy technology use. Make sure it is not dominating your own life before you begin to set standards and boundaries for your high schooler.

CONVERSATION STARTERS

- **WHAT IS YOUR FAVORITE APP (OR SOCIAL MEDIA PLATFORM)? WHY?** This answer may give you insight into what is popular among high schoolers and how your high schooler is using his technology. Try not to pass quick judgment on his response. You may need to spend some time researching the information he shares before you talk with him about what he's using.
- **WHAT ARE SOME OF THE DANGERS OF TECHNOLOGY?** It will be interesting to see if your high schooler is aware of how dangerous technology can be. If she is oblivious, find ways to highlight the dangers without condemnation.
- **WHAT ARE SOME WAYS TECHNOLOGY CAN BE USED FOR GOOD?** You don't want to always come across negative about technology. It is here to stay and will have a significant affect on all of our lives. Discuss things you could do as a family to use technology for good and the gospel.

SAY OR PRAY

- Pray that your high schooler would make wise choices about his use of technology.
- Pray your high schooler would find her value and significance in Christ, not in how many followers she has on social media.
- Pray that you would practice self-control when it comes to technology and be a good example of godly technology use.

BIG IDEA

Young adults should use technology in heatlthy, God-honoring ways.

KEY SCRIPTURES

- *We should be discerning when it comes to our use of technology* (1 Chron. 12:32).
- *We should reflect Christ in what we communicate online* (Prov. 17:27).
- *We should be above reproach with what we allow into our lives* (Ps. 101:1-3).
- *Nothing should be our master except Jesus* (1 Cor. 6:12).

KEY QUESTIONS YOUR YOUNG ADULT IS ASKING

- How can I gain more friends and followers on social media and become more significant?
- Why do I determine my self-worth on the basis of how many friends or followers I have or by how many likes I get on social media?
- How can I keep technology from dominating my life?
- Is social media all bad?

AT THIS AGE MOST YOUNG ADULTS WILL ...

- Have several ways to access the Internet.
- Be totally attached to their phones but will likely admit they spend too much time on them.
- Understand how social media can be used to leverage their social status.
- Be able to navigate several different social media platforms.

DEVELOPMENTAL MILESTONES

- With greater independence, young adults don't have as much, if any, parental restraints around their use of technology. They must self-discipline in this area.
- While young adults now have unlimited access to the Internet, they have to determine for themselves whether they will allow the Internet to have total access to them. They have the ability not to allow technology to dominate their lives.
- Young adults will continue to struggle with the consequences of what they post on social media or have posted in the past.

COACHING TIPS

- Young adults are still looking to their parents for guidance and examples of how they live. Since this is the case, make sure you're modeling Christ-honoring technology use. Don't send mixed messages, saying one thing, but practicing another.
- While there are many negative things about technology, there are ways it can be used for good. Initiate creative conversations about how technology can be used in positive ways, including how to use it to further the gospel.
- Remind your young adult that there are countless stories about people who didn't get jobs or lost their jobs because of remarks they made in emails or posted online. Caution your young adult to use restraint and carefully consider what he posts.
- Help your young adult understand how big a time waster technology can be. Point out how it can hinder her relationship with God, blind her from seeing people in need, and limit her in building meaningful relationships.
- While you don't have to use all the technology, try to stay abreast of what your young adult may be using, especially as it pertains to social media.
- Remember, if you pay the bill for your young adult's phone, you have the right to know what's on it and how it's being used.

CONVERSATION STARTERS

- **WHAT DO YOU SEE AS SOME DANGERS OF TECHNOLOGY?** It's easy to get pulled into the technological world without fully seeing the negatives. This conversation can be enlightening for you but can also help your young adult be more aware of the pitfalls of technology.
- **HOW CAN SOCIAL MEDIA BE CONSUMING?** This non-threatening question can easily lead to how social media is consuming them. This information may need to be read between the lines of what is actually said. Be discerning.
- **HOW ARE YOU SEEING TECHNOLOGY BEING USED FOR GOOD?** Discuss the positive uses of technology and how you both can honor God with your technology use.

SAY OR PRAY

- Pray your young adult will have Holy Spirit-led discernment in how he views and uses technology.
- Pray your young adult continues to find significance through her relationship with Christ, not on how many social media friends and followers she has.

LEADER GUIDE

LEADER TIPS

PRAY

Ask God to prepare you to lead this study. Pray individually and specifically for the parents in your group. Make this a priority in your personal walk and preparation.

PREPARE

SECURE PASTOR AND STAFF SUPPORT. You will need to talk with your pastor or staff if you want to teach this study as part of the ongoing ministry of your local church. Discuss together how it could best be used in your church. Ask for their input, prayers, and support.

SECURE YOUR LOCATION. Think about the number of people you can accommodate in the designated location. Reserve any tables, chairs, or media equipment for the videos, music, and additional audio needs.

PROVIDE CHILDCARE. This study is for parents. That means there are going to be children to be cared for. This is essential.

PROVIDE RESOURCES. Make sure you have a leader kit and the needed number of study books. You might get a few extra for any last-minute sign-ups.

PREVIEW EACH VIDEO SESSION. This will give you a grasp of the content and help prepare you for the Group Discussion. Look over the group discussion questions and consider your group of parents. Feel free to delete or reword the questions provided, and add other questions that fit the needs and circumstances of your group.

READ ALL THE ARTICLES AND AGE-GROUP MATERIAL. Use these as a guide to help prepare review questions for each group session.

KNOW YOUR GROUP. You're probably going to have a group of parents who will be in different stages of life with different ages of children. Keep this in mind as you prepare, especially if you keep all parents together in one large group. One option to consider is watching the video together as a large group, and then splitting into separate groups according to children's ages. If you choose this option, you will need to secure leadership for each small group.

INFORM

WARN OF SENSITIVE CONTENT. Inform your parents that the subject matter to be discussed may be uncomfortable and embarrassing at times. Just agree together that it will take place and put it aside. Agree to confidentiality. The group time needs to be a safe place to discuss difficult issues.

STAY HUMBLE. **Help parents understand that this is not a bragging session. Our tendency is to talk only about what we're doing right. Agree to have honest conversations with a willingness to discuss how we're struggling and even failing. Agree from the beginning that all of us struggle and fail.**

EVALUATE

After each session and throughout the study, assess what needs to be changed to more effectively lead the study.

STUDY ELEMENTS

OPEN. **Except for the first session, you will need to open each group session with a review of the previous week's teaching, especially the articles and age-group material. You will close this section of the study with a question that leads into the topic for the week.**

WATCH. **Each session has a 25- to 35-minute video that features a panel of parents discussing the topic of the session.**

DISCUSS. **Following the video, provide time for parents to discuss the session topic. We've provided questions to help you prompt and steer discussion. There are twelve discussion questions or prompts following each video. You probably will not be able to use all twelve. So be sure to review each session's questions to see which ones would best fit your group. Prioritize them. However, at the same time, be sensitive to the leading of the Holy Spirit in your group time. He may nudge you to go a different direction than you had planned.**

CLOSE. **The closing time will always offer at least one of the following elements:**

Encouragement. **You'll be given an encouraging and challenging word to share with parents as they depart.**

Prayer Moment. **This could be silent, individual, small group, or large group prayer.**

Takeaways. **Parents will be given an evaluative moment to determine the insight they have gleaned from the session and how they can apply it.**

Reminders. **Each week you will want to remind parents about the articles and age-group material that enhances or reinforces what was discussed on the video.**

TEACHING PLANS

SESSION 1: GOSPEL FRAMEWORK

OPEN

Welcome the parents to the first session of *Christ-Centered Parenting* and distribute the study books.

Begin the discussion by asking participants to name some parents depicted in past and current TV shows (examples: Andy Taylor, the Cleavers, the Bravermans, the Bradys, the Simpsons, etc.). Choose two or three of these fictional parents and briefly discuss their parenting style.

How would you rate your parenting against these TV parents? Explain.

Discuss how real-life parenting is difficult with lots of issues and questions, especially in the culture we live in today. Talk about how this six-week study will help parents be better equipped to parent in this day and time.

WATCH

Show the Session 1 video. Encourage parents to take notes on page 11.

DISCUSS

Use the questions provided in the Group Guide discussion section of the study book (pp. 12-13).

CLOSE

Direct attention to the Takeaways section on the Group Guide pages. Provide parents time to jot down a point or two of insight that they will take from this group session. Discuss briefly.

Point out the articles provided in Session 1. Explain that the articles will reinforce and enhance the issues discussed on the video. Encourage parents to read the articles and work through the reflection questions provided at the end of each article. Encourage them to discuss the reflection questions with their spouse or a trusted friend.

Point out the breakdown of the age-group material. Walk them through each section to help them understand the layout and content. Encourage them to peruse any section they like, but to pay close attention to the material on the current age-range of their children.

Lead your group in prayer to close the session.

SESSION 2: HUMAN DIGNITY

OPEN

Use the following questions to review the material from Session 1:

What are some things you learned from the articles? (Feel free as a leader to use some of the Questions for Reflection to foster discussion.)

What insights did you gain from the age-group material?

Ask and discuss the following question to turn attention toward the topic of this session:

What does it mean to be made in the image of God?

WATCH

Show the Session 2 video. Encourage parents to take notes on page 39.

DISCUSS

Use the questions provided in the Group Guide discussion section of the Bible study book (pp. 40-41).

CLOSE

Direct attention to the Takeaways section on the Group Guide pages. Provide parents time to jot down a point or two of insight that they will take from this group session. Discuss briefly.

Encourage parents to read the articles and age-group material that relate to this session.

Close with prayer.

SESSION 3: IDENTITY

OPEN

Use the following questions to review the material from Session 2:

What are some things you learned from the articles? (Feel free as a leader to use some of the Questions for Reflection to foster discussion.)

What insights did you gain from the age-group material?

Ask and discuss the following question to turn attention toward the topic of this session:

What were you taught about manhood and womanhood when you were growing up?

WATCH

Show the Session 3 video. Encourage parents to take notes on page 67.

DISCUSS

Use the questions provided in the Group Guide discussion section of the Bible study book (pp. 68-69).

CLOSE

Direct attention to the Takeaways section on the Group Guide pages. Provide parents time to jot down a point or two of insight that they will take from this group session. Discuss briefly.

Distribute index cards to parents. Instruct parents to write the name of their child(ren) on the cards, one child per card. Then under the child's name, write one prayer request they have for each child. After a few minutes, lead parents to get in small groups of three or four, share their requests, and pray for each others' children.

After groups have finished praying, remind parents about the articles and age-group material. Then close with prayer.

SESSION 4: SEXUALITY

OPEN

Use the following questions to review the material from Session 3:

What are some things you learned from the articles? (Feel free as a leader to use some of the Questions for Reflection to spur discussion.)

What insights did you gain from the age-group material?

Ask and discuss the following question to turn attention toward the topic of this session:

What are some of the sexual messages our children are currently receiving from the culture?

WATCH

Show the Session 4 video. Encourage parents to take notes on page 95.

DISCUSS

Use the questions provided in the Group Guide discussion section of the Bible study book (pp. 96-97).

CLOSE

Direct attention to the Takeaways section on the Group Guide pages. Provide parents time to jot down a point or two of insight that they will take from this group session. Discuss briefly.

Acknowledge that this subject is sometimes awkward and difficult to discuss with our children, but that it is an ongoing conversation we must have with them. Encourage parents to get in small groups, share concerns they have about this subject, and then pray for each other.

After groups have finished praying, remind parents about the articles and age-group material. Then close with prayer.

SESSION 5: RELATIONSHIPS

OPEN

Use the following questions to review the material from Session 4:

What are some things you learned from the articles? (Feel free as a leader to use some of the Questions for Reflection to spur discussion.)

What insights did you gain from the age-group material?

Ask and discuss the following question to turn attention toward the topic of this session:

What did you learn about marriage, both positive and negative, from your parents?

WATCH

Show the Session 5 video. Encourage parents to take notes on page 123.

DISCUSS

Use the questions provided in the Group Guide discussion section of the Bible study book (pp. 124-125).

CLOSE

Direct attention to the Takeaways section on the Group Guide pages. Provide parents time to jot down a point or two of insight that they will take from this group session. Discuss briefly.

Provide an opportunity for parents to share prayer concerns and requests they have for their families. As a request is named, ask for a volunteer to stand and pray for that specific request. As the leader, intercede on behalf of all the families to close the session.

As you dismiss, remind parents about the articles and age-group material.

SESSION 6: TECHNOLOGY

OPEN

Use the following questions to review the material from Session 5:

What are some things you learned from the articles? (Feel free as a leader to use some of the Questions for Reflection to spur discussion.)

What insights did you gain from the age-group material?

Ask and discuss the following question to turn attention toward the topic of this session:

How many technological devices do you have in your home? Are you surprised by that number? Why or why not?

WATCH

Show the Session 6 video. Encourage parents to take notes on page 151.

DISCUSS

Use the questions provided in the Group Guide discussion section of the Bible study book (pp. 152-153).

CLOSE

Instruct parents to take a few minutes to look back through their books and determine a few things they have heard or learned that has changed the way they parent their child. Also ask them to determine something they learned that they have yet to implement. They can list their answers in the Takeaways section of the Group Guide. After a few minutes, allow parents to share their findings.

Remind parents that though this may be the last video session, they still have articles and age-group material to read and review during the week ahead.

Prior to the session, compile a list of all the parents who have attended the class. Make copies of the list and distribute one copy to each parent or set of parents as you close the session. Encourage them to use this list as a reminder to pray for each other as they attempt to parent their children in a Christ-centered way.

Pray and dismiss.

SESSION 7 (OPTIONAL)

Because parents have articles and age-group material following the last video, you may choose to conduct a seventh session in order to review and discuss the Session 6 material.

OPEN

Use the following questions to review the material from Session 6:

What are some things you learned from the articles? (Feel free as a leader to use some of the Questions for Reflection to spur discussion.)

What insights did you gain from the age-group material?

DISCUSS

Since there is no video to view, use the following questions to debrief the whole study.

Of the six areas we dealt with—gospel framework, human dignity, identity, sexuality, relationships, and technology—which one currently seems to be the most difficult to deal with as a parent? Explain.

Which session material and discussion has impacted you the most? In what ways?

In the opening of the very first video, Russell Moore said parenting is spiritual warfare. Do you agree with his statement? Explain. How has this study better equipped you to fight this battle?

If you had the opportunity to tell a set of brand new parents one important thing about parenting, what would it be?

CLOSE

Provide index cards for your group. Instruct each parent to write and fill in the following statements on a card:

My greatest fear as a parent is ...

My greatest joy as a parent is ...

My greatest need as a parent is ...

After a few minutes, break into small groups and instruct parents to share what's on their cards. Provide time for parents to pray for each other in their small groups. Then encourage them to trade cards with each other and use those cards as a reminder to pray for each other in the days ahead. Lead the group in a closing prayer as you dismiss.

ENDNOTES

WEEK 1

1. R. Albert Mohler, *We Cannot Be Silent: Speaking Truth to a Culture Redefining Sex, Marriage, and the Very Meaning of Right and Wrong* (Nashville, TN: Nelson Books, 2015), 1.
2. Samuel James. "The Culture War Is Interested in You," (May 18, 2016). Available at https://mereorthodoxy.com.
3. Chap Bettis, *The Disciple-Making Parent: A Comprehensive Guidebook for Raising Your Children to Love and Follow Jesus Christ* (Diamond Hill Publishing, 2016), 7.
4. Andy Crouch, *Culture Making: Recovering Our Creative Calling* (Downers Grove, IL: IVP Books, 2008), 12.
5. J.D. Greear, *The Gospel and Same-Sex Marriage* (Nashville, TN: B&H Publishing, 2016), 72.
6. Adapted from Daniel Darling, "Five Common Mistakes Christian Parents Make," accessed 1 Oct. 2016. Available at www.danieldarling.com.
7. David E. Prince. "Raising Courageous Kids," accessed 1 Oct. 2016. Available at http://erlc.com.

WEEK 2

1. Russell Moore, "How the Gospel Shapes the Sanctity of Life," ERLC.com, published Jan. 26, 2016, accessed May 1, 2017. Available at http://erlc.com.
2. Ibid.
3. "September 2016 Fact Sheet," Guttmacher Institute, accessed May 1, 2017. Available at www.guttmacher.org.
4. Steven Ertelt, "57,762,169 Abortions in America Since Roe vs. Wade in 1973," LifeNews.com, published Jan. 21, 2015. Available at www.life-news.com.
5. Lydia Saad, "Generational Differences on Abortion Narrow," Gallup.com, published March 12, 2010. Available at www.gallup.com.
6. Adapted from Russell Moore, "The Gospel vs 100 Years of Planned Parenthood," published Oct. 17, 2016, accessed May 1, 2017. Available at www.russellmoore.com.
7. Trillia J. Newbell, *United: Captured by God's Vision for Diversity* (Chicago, IL: Moody Publishers, 2014), 63.
8. Eric Mason, "How Should the Church Engage?" *The Gospel for Life Series: The Gospel & Racial Reconciliation* (Nashville, TN: B&H Publishing, 2016), 59.
9. Daniel J. Hurst, "Physician-Assisted Suicide and Euthanasia: A Slippery Slope Indeed," Canon & Culture, published July 29, 2015, accessed Dec. 31, 2016. Available at www.canonandculture.com.
10. Joe Carter, "5 Facts About Physician Assisted Suicide in America," Erlc.com, published Oct. 8, 2015, accessed Dec. 31, 2016. Available at http://erlc.com.

WEEK 3

1. John Piper, *A Holy Ambition: To Preach Where Christ Has Not Been Named, A Collection of Sermons by John Piper* (Minneapolis: Desiring God Foundation, 2011), 41.
2. David Prince, "Youth Sports and the Everyone Wins Mentality," Erlc.com, published Oct. 12, 2015, accessed Jan. 20, 2017. Available at http://erlc.com.
3. Matt Chandler, *A Beautiful Design* (Nashville: LifeWay Press, 2016), 47.
4. Russell Moore, *Questions and Ethics: Applying the Gospel to Tough Situations* (Nashville, TN: Leland House Press, 2014), Kindle Edition.

5. Ibid.

6. Jared Kennedy, "The Kids Are Not All Right: How to Help Teens Who Are Anxious and Depressed," published Dec. 12, 2016, accessed Jan. 29, 2017. Available at http://erlc.com.

7. "For Parents and Caregivers," Mentalhealth. gov, accessed Jan. 29, 2017, www. mentalhealth.gov.

8. American Foundation for Suicide Prevention, accessed Jan. 29, 2017. Available at https://afsp.org.

9. The Jason Foundation, "Youth Suicide Statistics," accessed Jan. 29, 2017. Available at http://jasonfoundation.com.

WEEK 4

1. David Platt, "A Gospel Approach to Homosexuality, Singleness, and Marriage," Erlc.com, published Oct. 30, 2014. Accessed Jan. 25, 2017. Available at http://erlc.com.

2. Dean Inserra, "Dating Wisely," DeanInserra.com, published Sept. 17, 2014. Accessed Jan. 11, 2017. Available at http://deaninserra.com.

3. J.D. Greear, "How Should the Church Engage?" *The Gospel for Life Series: The Gospel & Same-Sex Marriage* (Nashville, TN: B&H Publishing, 2016), 77.

4. Adapted from Russell Moore, "Ashley Madison Is Just the Beginning," RussellMoore.com, published Sept. 3, 2015. Accessed Jan. 11, 2017. Available at www.russellmoore.com.

5. Garrett Kell, "12 Observations After Reading the Porn Phenomenon," Erlc.com, published Aug. 3, 2016. Accessed Jan. 30, 2017. Available at http://erlc.com.

6. William M. Struthers, *Wired for Intimacy: How Pornography Hijacks the Male Brain* (Downers Grove, IL: InterVarsity Press, 2009), 48.

7. "Girls Addicted to Porn," *The Wire*, Parenting Teens, p. 4.

8. "Protect Your Family. Stop Porn." CovenantEyes.com. Accessed May 4, 2017. Available at covenanteyes.com/pornstats.

WEEK 5

1. David Platt in "A Gospel Approach to Homosexuality, Singleness, and Marriage," Erlc.com, published Oct. 30, 2014, accessed Jan 25, 2017. Available at http://erlc.com.

2. Mary Kassian, *The Gospel for Life Series: The Gospel & Marriage* (Nashville, TN: B&H Publishing, 2017), 7.

3. Andrew T. Walker and Eric Teetsel, *Marriage Is: How Marriage Transforms Society and Cultivates Human Flourishing* (Nashville, TN: B&H Publishing, 2015), Kindle Edition, Locations 517-522.

4. Ibid, Kassian, *The Gospel & Marriage*, 20.

5. Sam Allberry, *Connected: Living in the Light of the Trinity* (Phillipsburg, New Jersey: P&R Publishing, 2013), 127.

6. Ibid, Walker and Teetsel, *Marriage Is*, Kindle Edition, Location 430.

7. Ibid, Kassian, *The Gospel & Marriage*, 20.

8. Wendy Wang and Kim Parker, "Chapter 4: Never-Married Young Adults on the Marriage Market," PewSocialTrends.org, published Sept. 24, 2014, accessed Jan. 27, 2017. Available at www.pewsocialtrends.org.

9. Wang and Parker, March 2013 Current Population Survey, "Record Share of Americans Have Never Married," PewSocialTrends.org, published Sept. 24, 2014, accessed Jan. 27, 2017. Available at www.pewsocialtrends.org.

10. Andrew T. Walker, *The Gospel for Life Series: The Gospel & Marriage* (Nashville, TN: B&H Publishing, 2017), 87-88.

11. Ibid.

12. Russell Moore, "How Should You Talk to Your Children About Same-Sex Marriage?" RussellMoore.com, accessed

Jan. 27, 2017. Available at www.russellmoore.com.

13. Moore, podcast "Questions & Ethics: My Daughter Is Having a Same-Sex Wedding-Now What?" RussellMoore.com, published Sept. 8, 2015, accessed Jan. 30, 2017. Available at www.russellmoore.com.

14. Dean Inserra, "Dating Wisely," DeanInserra.com, published Sept 17, 2014, accessed Jan 9, 2017. Available at http://deaninserra.com.

15. Ibid.

16. Ibid.

WEEK 6

1. Russell Moore, "Smartphones, Tablets, and Christian Parenting," RussellMoore.com, published June 2, 2015, accessed Jan. 15, 2017. Available at www.russellmoore.com.

2. Brian Housman, interview by Dennis Rainey and Bob Lepine, "Developing a Theology of Technology," FamilyLife Today Radio Transcript, Mar. 23, 2015. Available at http://familylifetoday.com.

3. Brian Housman, interview by Dennis Rainey and Bob Lepine, "Internet Safety Tips," FamilyLife Today Radio Transcript, March 24, 2015. Available at http://familylifetoday.com.

4. "What Parents Should Know About Sexting (Part 1)," Erlc.com, published Dec. 2, 2014, accessed Jan. 28, 2017. Available at http://erlc.com.

5. "The Snappening is Happening: 5 Ways to Talk to Your Teens About Sexting," Erlc.com, published Oct. 28, 2014, accessed Jan. 28, 2017. Available at http://erlc.com.

6. "Porn Sites Get More Visitors Each Month Than Netflix, Amazon And Twitter Combined," The Huffington Post, published May 4, 2013, accessed May 10, 2017. Available at www.huffingtonpost.com.

7. Russell Moore, "Transcript: Should I Let My Twelve-Year-Old Have a Smartphone?"

Erlc.com, accessed Jan. 15, 2017. Available at http://erlc.com.

8. Allyson Hepp, "5 Health Benefits of Playing Outside," Care.com, accessed Dec. 4, 2016. Available at www.care.com/c/stories/4178/5-health-benefits-of-playing-outside/.

9. Vicki Courtney, "3 Ways to Help Your Daughter Find Her Worth in Christ," Erlc.com, published Nov. 21, 2016, accessed Jan. 15, 2017. Available at http://erlc.com.

10. Erin Davis, "Teenagers and Technology: 3 Things You Might Be Missing," Erlc.com, published July 31, 2015, accessed Jan. 15, 2017. Available at http://erlc.com.

ABOUT THE ERLC

The Ethics & Religious Liberty Commission is dedicated to engaging the culture with the gospel of Jesus Christ and speaking to issues in the public square for the protection of religious liberty and human flourishing.

Since its inception, the ERLC has been defined around a holistic vision of the kingdom of God, leading the culture to change within the church itself and then as the church addresses the world.

MISSION

The Ethics & Religious Liberty Commission exists to assist the churches by helping them understand the moral demands of the gospel, apply Christian principles to moral and social problems and questions of public policy, and to promote religious liberty in cooperation with the churches and other Southern Baptist entities.

MINISTRIES

The Ethics & Religious Liberty Commission exists to assist the churches by helping:

- Apply the moral and ethical teachings of the Bible to the Christian life.

- Through the communication and advocacy of moral and ethical concerns in the public arena.

- In their moral witness in local communities.

- Promote religious liberty.

RELATIONSHIPS

The Ethics & Religious Liberty Commission will work within the Southern Baptist Convention agency relationship guidelines approved by the Inter-Agency Council and the Executive Committee and printed in the Organization Manual of the Southern Baptist Convention.

THE ETHICS & RELIGIOUS
LIBERTY COMMISSION
OF THE SOUTHERN BAPTIST CONVENTION